# Quilts
## IN THE ATTIC

By Karen S. Musgrave

Editor: Melinda Keefe
Design Manager: LeAnn Kuhlmann
Layout by: Erin Fahringer
Cover designed by: Rick Korab

Printed in China

Photo credits:

Back cover, © Allen Lee Lake/Shutterstock
p. 34, © Danita Delimont/Alamy
p. 43, © Marie C. Fields/Shutterstock
p. 101, © LorenRyePhoto/Alamy
p. 109, © brt PHOTO/Alamy
p. 123, © Frances M. Roberts/Alamy
p. 135, © Doug Wilson/Alamy
p. 147, © Andre Jenny/Alamy

# CONTENTS

| | |
|---|---|
| *Introduction* | 4 |
| Nellie's Beauty | 8 |
| Wandering Foot | 16 |
| An Unexpected Gift | 22 |
| The Oldest UFO | 30 |
| Elizabeth | 38 |
| Crazy All This Time | 46 |
| A Quilt in Three Pieces | 54 |
| A French Bed | 62 |
| History Returned | 72 |
| A Locked Door Changes Everything | 80 |
| Moonlight Magic | 88 |
| One Word | 96 |
| Sarah Frances | 106 |
| Sunday School Picnic | 114 |
| Ladies Reading Circle | 124 |
| A Forgotten Quilt | 132 |
| Old Maid, New Woman | 140 |
| History Divided | 150 |
| The Doctor and the Quiltmaker | 158 |
| Reproducing the Past, Touching the Present | 166 |
| How Hard Could It Be? | 174 |
| Joe the Quilter | 180 |
| Mary Moon, Who Were You? | 188 |
| In Honor of Harriett | 196 |
| Eye of Panic | 204 |
| Legacy Reclaimed | 212 |
| A Blessing and an Affirmation | 222 |
| A Gift for Eleanor | 230 |
| The Westward Trail of Sarah Snouffer's Quilt | 236 |
| I Will | 246 |
| *Acknowledgments* | 255 |

# INTRODUCTION

When Margret Aldrich of Voyageur Press inquired if I was interested in writing a book about quilt discoveries, my first thought was "This book was made for me." I was fortunate to grow up surrounded by gifted storytellers. I remember sneaking out of my bedroom to eavesdrop on the adults on Friday nights when my aunts and uncles gathered at my house. As a child, I was that kid who asked "why" to the point of making teachers and my mom crazy. My mom tried using the saying "Curiosity killed the cat" to stop me, until I discovered that the saying had an ending—"And satisfaction brought her back"—which still rings true to me. And while quilts were never a part of my life as a child, I was drawn to them early. I made my first quilt while still in high school, beginning a lifelong love affair.

I loved interviewing and getting to know the people involved in each of these essays. I feel a deep connection to the quiltmakers, and it is my hope that you will, too. I adored the research, made so much easier these days with the Internet. I worked on the writing even when I was asleep. It was glorious.

Of course, this would not have been possible without the open hearts of the people who shared their stories and lives with me and answered hundreds of questions. (Your secrets are safe with me, and your hearts will always be close to mine.)

Often, the stories in this book had been passed down through the generations, with facts being lost or muddled. The romanticizing of quilts also adds another layer of complication. I tried to be as respectful and factual as possible. The facts were often much more compelling than the fantasy. Often, in my research, I would unravel a mystery or discover a missing piece to a story. I found places where family was buried; I found the births and deaths of unknown relatives. Too often, I could not be certain of the actual maker of the quilt, but that does not change the impact a quilt had on families, often through many generations.

The stories told here really do show the basic drive in the human spirit to create something that carries purpose and meaning. They also give us a unique glimpse into our history. *Old Maid, New Woman* sheds light on a time in the 1880s when it was not uncommon for women to declare they would not marry. With *A Gift for Eleanor*, we learn about the Jews of South Carolina in the early 1850s and a slave named Rinah. In *History Divided*, a highly observant guest changes how a silk Quaker quilt is viewed and understood. With *I Will*, we delve into the 1933 World's Fair's Century of Progress International Exposition, with the Sears National Quilt Contest. Two stories involve the returning of a quilt to the place it was made: *Crazy All This Time* is about a 121-year-old crazy quilt donated to a high school in Waterville, Maine, and *History Returned* deals with a fund-raising signature quilt returned to Merna, Nebraska. *A French Bed* takes us to France and a twelfth-century castle.

There are modern-day stories, too. *An Unexpected Gift* involves a famous quiltmaker from the 1980s who is now a Buddhist living in the Himalayan Mountains in Darjeeling, India. *Reproducing the Past, Touching the Present* deals with the challenges of reproducing an antique quilt. The healing aspects of making a quilt are part of *Eye of Panic*. The story of *Mary Moon, Who Were You?* not only shares the brief life of Mary Moon, but how her quilt influenced multimedia artist and writer Lynne Perrella. *Joe the Quilter* is actually about two Joes who quilt—one born in England in 1750 and the other born in 1953 and living today in California.

There are stories for which I tried desperately to find more information without success. I would love to know more about the Pine Tree Club mentioned in *How Hard Could It Be?* or how Mary Moon died. Or why the incredible quilt in *A Quilt in Three Pieces* was divided. Or what happened to Rinah in *A Gift for Eleanor*.

I am happy that there are two stories, *The Doctor and the Quiltmaker* and *Legacy Reclaimed*, that share the lives of two pioneering businesswomen and history makers—Marie Webster and Ruby Short McKim—who lived and worked at the same time. There are stories that involve Julie Silber (*A Forgotten Quilt*) and Shelly Zegart (*Sunday School Picnic* and *Old Maid, New Woman*). Both of these women have made major contributions to the world of quilts. There are two stories, *One Word* and *In Honor of Harriett,* about quilts in the collection of the International Quilt Study Center and Museum, University of Nebraska–Lincoln. *A Locked Door Changes Everything* informs us, as the title says, of how a locked door changes the life of Gee's Bend quiltmaker Mary Lee Bendolph.

Though the makers of the quilts probably did not set out to touch our feelings, longings, and lives, there is something universal in their stories. I am thrilled to share with you these subtle, thoughtful, and sometimes humorous stories. ❧

# NETTIE'S BEAUTY

Nettie Miller Sours was found dead in her bed with her hands neatly crossed on her chest—a true Virginia mountain woman to the end. It was January 20, 1968, and she was ninety years old—the seventh and last child of John Miller and Sarah Pettit Miller.

Her roots had run deep in the Shenandoah Valley, which is both a geographic and cultural region of western Virginia and West Virginia. After the death of her husband, Charles, in 1949, Nettie did not move in with her son, Lawrence, but lived alone in the family home with no central heat, cooking in a kitchen with a sub–ground floor on a wood-burning stove. The rooms were small, the ceilings low (about five feet six inches), and the hall and stairways were very narrow. The outhouse was fifty yards behind the house.

When asked, Nettie's family members thought her best trait was her personality. Nettie was a petite woman who loved

---

*Nettie's Beauty*
Feathered Star variation
Possibly made by Nettie Miller Sours (1878–1968) or her mother,
    Sarah Pettit Miller, Virginia
Circa late nineteenth century
80 x 72 inches
Cotton; hand pieced and hand quilted
*Collection of Karen Alexander, photo by Barbara Tricarico*

to tell stories and to laugh, often covering her mouth with her ever-present apron. She always had a large vegetable garden and was legendary for her skilled use of a whip. Robert, her great-great-nephew, remembered her as a tough and independent woman. If she discovered a snake in her garden, she would "get her whip and snap the critter in two." When Robert's mother would write Nettie and tell her she was coming to visit, Nettie would often request a piece of fresh fish and a pint of whiskey.

In 1962, the local paper, the *Page News and Courier*, featured an article about nearly eighty-four-year-old Nettie and her "handmade carpets," which she made on a loom that originally belonged to her great-great-grandmother and was housed in one of the farm's outbuildings. She was still selling her woven rag rugs to people across the country at that time.

*Nettie always had a large vegetable garden and was legendary for her skilled use of a whip.*

While Karen Alexander had not grown up in the Shenandoah Valley, her family roots there go back to 1740, and she learned to quilt and began studying quilt history in 1979 while living in Virginia. So on a warm June day in 1998, Karen headed off to an estate auction in Luray (an hour and a half from her Reston home) that she had seen advertised in her local newspaper. The public auction was to settle the estate of Lawrence R. Sours, who had died childless in April, and the listing of "quilts" had caught her eye.

It was only her sixth auction in three years, but she had learned a thing or two. Walking through a maze of items spread across the farm's lawn—green Depression glass, crocks, pots and pans, two wringer washers, chicken coops, carpentry and woodworking tools, a treadle sewing machine, a 1966 Chevrolet pickup truck with less than 22,000 miles on the speedometer—her heart leapt when she saw ten or twelve quilts stretched on two long clotheslines, dancing in the breeze. One bold quilt kept peeking out and catching her eye. It was breathtaking and so different from the others. "It appeared to be playing hide-and-seek with the others. So dull in contrast to this beauty's flash, the other quilts appeared to be guardians." She tried hard to contain her excitement and did not wish to tip her hand by letting others know that she was interested. She made herself wait a long twenty minutes before approaching the quilts and occupied her time taking photographs of different items for sale. It also helped belay any suspicions of interest when she took photographs of all of the quilts.

When she was finally able to make a closer inspection, her beliefs about the quilt were confirmed, making it even harder for her to contain her excitement about this great find. It appeared to be a "special" quilt because the fabrics were bright and clear, indicating that it was probably seldom used if, in fact, ever washed. There were a few stains that could have been made from contact with the oil from wood over the years, but these stains were small and did not impact the visual beauty of the quilt. Its double pink, cheddar orange, rust, moss green, and cadet blue fabrics reminded Karen of the bright folk art paintings with the Pennsylvania Dutch look that could be found in the Shenandoah Valley.

The late nineteenth-century fabrics in the quilt were much older than the fabrics in the other quilts. The pattern was a variation of a Feathered Star with sixteen 14½-inch by 14½-inch hand pieced blocks. The hand pieced sashing between the blocks was 5 inches wide, with a square surrounded by triangles where the sashing met. The pieced backing was a black-and-white checked fabric that had been turned to the front for a ¼-inch binding. The quilting was simple but well done with ten to twelve stitches to the inch. The batting was thin cotton. It was approximately 80 inches by 72 inches. None of the other quilts were as intricately made. What was the story here?

The auction drew distant family members to the farm that day, which caused much reminiscing and sharing. The family had a long lineage of quiltmakers, including some of Nettie's nieces. Karen spent some time interviewing the family about the quilt and its maker. They all believed that the quilt was made by Lawrence Sours's mother, Nettie Miller Sours. All Karen knew was that she had to own this quilt!

Karen's budget would only allow her to pay at most $400, but she knew in her heart that she was prepared to go as high as $500. Could she win? Auctions often have a "quilt picker" present, a person who will only buy a quilt if it can be quickly resold for a nice profit. Karen felt that there was at least one picker in the crowd. The bidding began fast and furiously among five people. Two people dropped out quickly. Another one of the bidders, who Karen thought was a picker, dropped out when the bid hit $250. However, Karen hadn't won yet.

In the crowd, standing behind Karen, was a woman pushing up the bid. With sweating palms and a thudding heart, Karen kept her eyes on the prize, not daring to look at the woman, whom she suspected was related to Nettie. While she did not want to cause offense or pain, she *really* had to have that quilt. As quickly as it started, the bidding was over, with a final bid of $375. Karen was stunned. She had won! Several people offered congratulations. Karen could not believe it. She easily would have gone to $500.

Earlier in the day, one of the cousins had pointed out to Karen with great pride a book that contained a newspaper clipping with two photos of Nettie. One photo showed Nettie working at her loom, and the other showed her holding one of the rag rugs she had made. The article said that Nettie had been "famous" in the valley for her rag rug weaving, not her quiltmaking, and Karen desperately wanted the article for her documentation. As the auction continued to drag on and on, Karen realized that she would not be able to stick around to bid on one of Nettie's rugs or the box of books containing the newspaper article. Feeling bold, Karen decided to seek out the executor of the estate, Elizabeth Gochenour, and make an outrageous request. Could she have the newspaper clipping, or at least a copy of it, because she could not stay any longer? After Karen explained to Elizabeth that she had purchased one of Nettie's quilts, Elizabeth asked to see it, after which she happily handed over the clipping. As Karen left with her treasures, several people made it a point to tell her goodbye. Karen felt she had come as a stranger but was leaving as part of the family.

With the newspaper clipping and notes from her interviews, she continued to research the genealogy archives at the Page County Library to learn more about Nettie and her family. She also maintained contact with family members through correspondence and telephone calls. In 2000, she received an e-mail from a great-great-niece of Nettie's, who told her that some family members believed the quilt was made by Nettie's mother, Sarah. (Oral history is not always reliable, but given that the fabrics in the quilt were made within the decade in which Nettie was born, this seems likely. However, the fabrics could have been passed on to Nettie from her mother, or Nettie could have made the quilt in her early teens using fabrics from her mother's scrap bag.) Karen further discovered that Sarah had grown up in Pine Grove Hollow just above Karen's great-grandfather's home on Hawksbill Creek. These connections made the quilt even more meaningful to her.

Karen came to call the quilt *Nettie's Beauty*. She does not use the quilt to sleep under. Instead, the quilt is laid out on her queen-size guest bed for a couple of months at a time, then folded and stacked for a couple of months along with Karen's other Virginia Valley quilts: ten full-size, one doll-size, and one crib-size. Karen also has used *Nettie's Beauty* as part of a lecture she gives to interested groups and organizations on Virginia Valley quilts.

*Nettie's Beauty* was shown in 2001 at the American Quilt Study Group conference in Williamsburg, Virginia; in 2003 at Celebrate Fairfax in an exhibition called *Hands On History: Quilts of Virginia* in Fairfax, Virginia; and in 2005 at Indiana

Wesleyan University, Beard Arts Center, in an exhibition called *Stitches Saved in Time* in Marion, Indiana. Karen remains willing to have the quilt in future exhibitions. Even though she left Virginia and now lives in Washington State, someday she plans to offer the quilt and supporting materials to a Virginia museum.

We may never know for certain who made *Nettie's Beauty*, but as long as we share the story of Nettie Miller Sours and Sarah Pettit Miller, they will not be forgotten.

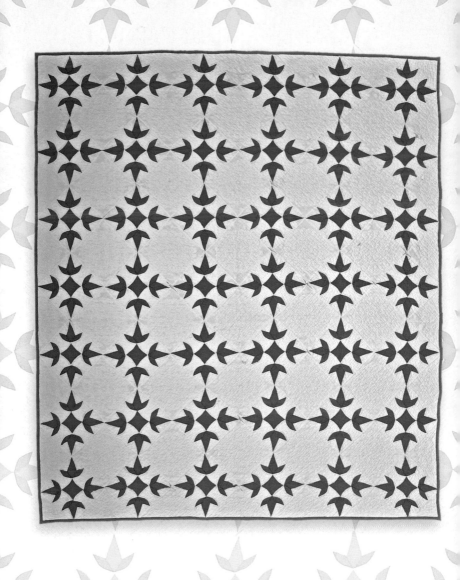

# WANDERING FOOT

Her painful childhood should have broken Delores Hamilton, and in a way, it did. However, the love of one grandmother (along with a quilt she made) eventually brought some understanding. In 1940, that grandmother, Mary Smith, known to everyone as Molly, presented her son, Foster, and his wife, Estel, with a red, white, and blue Turkey Track (sometimes called Wandering Foot) quilt as a wedding gift. It's not known if it was a "shotgun wedding," but it is possible, since Estel was two months pregnant. Everyone in the farm community of Leon (located in southern Iowa near the Missouri border) was a good shot—even Molly, who owned a few shotguns. Shotgun weddings, with actual shotguns, justices of the peace, and grooms being rousted out of bed at midnight, were not unusual in this time and place. And while it was a marriage that lasted more than sixty-five years, it was never a happy one.

Estel, having lived through the Great Depression, hated all things handmade and quilts in particular, so she kept her

Turkey Tracks or Wandering Foot
Made by Mary "Molly" Smith, Leon, Iowa
1940
Originally 82 x 92 inches, now 58 x 68 inches (borders were removed)
Cotton; hand pieced and hand quilted
*Collection of Delores Hamilton, photo by Delores Hamilton*

mother-in-law's gift stuffed in a closet in every house they called home. Foster had absolutely no interest in anything to do with "women's work," which included the quilt. This was pretty much the norm in the poor, blue-collar neighborhoods where they lived. One of the homes the family lived in was only 400 square feet with a tiny linen closet, with room only for a few towels and toiletries. Bedding was washed, hung on the clothesline to dry, and put back onto the beds. The home's half closet, which was between the home's two bedrooms, had a hole in it that was eventually stuffed closed with the quilt.

Delores, the couple's only child at the time, had noticed that something was stuffed into the hole, but it wasn't until she was around nine that her curiosity got the better of her. She fished out what was blocking the hole, but she obeyed her mother and didn't crawl through the hole. Her presence in her parents' bedroom was strictly forbidden. When she pulled out the object, she discovered it was a quilt and instantly fell in love with it. She knew none of its history, and she knew that she could not ask any questions about it. So she opened it, sat on it, rolled up in it, then promptly put it back, all the while staying inside her half closet.

As long as she was quiet, her mother rarely checked on her, so this activity was safe. After playing with the quilt, she would always stuff it back into the hole. This secret quilt enjoyment went on until Delores was eleven. On a cold night in 1952, she decided to put it on her bed to provide needed warmth. As usual, the coal in the furnace had run out in the middle of the night, and Iowa winters are bitterly cold. The next morning, when her mother woke her and saw the quilt on the bed, she immediately became enraged. It was then that she shared with her daughter how much she hated the quilt and the woman who made it. It was the first time Delores realized that her mother hated her grandmother, whom Delores loved so dearly.

When her mother's tirade ended, a stunned Delores gently folded the quilt and stuffed it back into the hole, but each night after, she pulled it out and snuggled with it on her bed, making sure to put it back before her morning wake-up call. To Delores's surprise, right before the family moved to Los Angeles, her mother allowed Delores to take full possession of the quilt. However, there were stipulations. Delores could not display it on top of her bed. Instead, it had to be turned facedown, then covered with a cheap chenille bedcover that she never liked. Her mother never wanted to see the quilt. Delores dutifully complied, yet the quilt stayed on her bed even during the year's hot months, never stuffed in a closet again.

The colors certainly are patriotic, but no one knows why Molly chose them. The quilt is handpieced, with precision in the curves, and the hand quilting, which does not have particularly small stitches, is even and precise. The back is the same white cotton fabric that is on the front. Originally it had 12-inch borders, but when they began to become tattered, Delores cut them off and bound the quilt with store-bought packaged cotton binding. Not being a quiltmaker at the time, Delores knew nothing about how to properly care for a quilt. The cotton filler is reduced to tiny, very hard balls of cotton that can no longer be called batting, and some of the fabrics are so thin that they cannot be repaired any further. This quilt has been through the wringer, literally and figuratively, so many times that it is surprising how much of it has survived since

1940. "I had no idea how to properly care for a quilt, so I was probably the wrong person to take it under my wing," Delores says. "But no one could have loved it more." Delores uses it as a lap quilt and plans to continue using it until none of it is left.

In 1973, Delores made her first bed quilt for her daughter, long before she knew what she was doing and long before she had any formal training. She began taking quilt classes and making quilts in earnest in 1988, and being somewhat of a class junkie, she has taken at least five classes every year since. She's even taken quilt classes on a cruise. While Delores began by creating traditional quilts, she now makes art quilts, and for her, making quilts has become "my passion, my love, my fervent calling in life."

Generally, superstitions and myths surrounding quilts should be taken with a grain of salt or simply for fun, but Delores Hamilton isn't so sure about that, because when she discovered the Wandering Foot pattern her grandmother had used and read up on it, the quilt she loved took on a deeper meaning.

According to legend, if a boy or a man slept under a Wandering Foot quilt, he would someday wander westward, leaving his mother or his bride behind. Delores also believes that the superstition also meant that a husband might wander into another woman's bed. Apparently, the curse on this type of quilt was lifted by changing the name of the pattern to Turkey Tracks. The gift of a quilt with this particular pattern was either Molly's big *faux pas* or a clear message that she knew her son all too well. Delores believes it was the latter because Molly was a wise woman and because Molly's son did, indeed, "wander."

The affair happened shortly after Delores was born, a fact her mother shared with her when she was quite young, but she would never name the woman. In 2005, after her father died, Delores's cousin called to extend her sympathy. It quickly became apparent that the real reason for the call was to find out if Delores knew the family secret about her dad. She did not. It turns out that the woman Foster had the affair with shortly after his marriage was Estel's younger (and much more beautiful) sister. And, to make matters worse, her aunt had gotten pregnant from the affair.

This was her aunt's second out-of-wedlock pregnancy, which the family quaintly referred to as her "situation." She had put the first child, a boy, up for adoption, as was customary in those days. There was no mention of the father, but apparently, he was not Foster. The second child, a girl named Nora, she was allowed to keep because her mother, who was deeply religious, felt that the child, being born on Christmas Day, was a gift from God. Nora was a smart, beautiful child with a devilish streak who, in her Grandmother Molly's eyes, could do no wrong.

When her cousin finished sharing the news, Delores's first comment was that she had always wanted a sister or brother. Being an only child had been an extremely unpleasant experience for her. Unfortunately, she had lost track of Nora after they had played together at Grandmother Molly's house during their childhood, so there would be no reconnection.

Delores Hamilton experienced alienation from her parents, felt sorrow and loss, and knew the failure of two marriages of her own. And yet, she is a person with empathy, compassion, and thoughtfulness, as well as a great sense of humor. She says, "I will always love the quilt. But not once did I ever put that quilt on the bed that either of my two husbands slept in. I'm no fool." ❧

# AN UNEXPECTED GIFT

In 2010, a quiet moment in the Oregon Quilt Project's tent at the thirty-fifth annual Sisters Outdoor Quilt Show in Sisters, Oregon, was broken when a rather diminutive woman in her mid-sixties wearing simple Asian clothing walked into the tent. Her gray hair was pulled back into a ponytail. She wore no makeup. An aura of wisdom and peace seemed to radiate from her, which seemed almost at odds with her underlying sense of purpose. She urgently needed to find a home for one of her quilts.

She explained that she had once been involved in the world of quilts and had even published a book. The quilt she had brought with her had been included in the prestigious Quilt National exhibition in 1983 in Athens, Ohio. She had considered selling it or donating it to a museum, but she had dismissed those options because she did not want to be involved in the long processes they required. The quilt's financial value did not seem to matter to her, but she clearly

---

*Night Flight*
Made by Andrea Leong Scadden, Seattle, Washington
1982
62 x 69 inches
Cotton and cotton polyester; machine pieced and hand quilted
*Collection of Bill Volckening, photo by Bill Volckening*

wanted it to be preserved and maintained. She shared that she was now a recluse, living in the Himalayan Mountains in Darjeeling, India.

The crowd of volunteers looked on with disbelief, mouths open, trying to make sense of all that she had said. Bill Volckening, Oregon Quilt Project coordinator, finally understood and blurted out, "I love free quilts and I'd be happy to give it a good home!" This seemed to make the woman happy. After exchanging some information, she walked away, only to reappear about thirty minutes later with not one but two quilts, as well as a book and some documents.

Before the encounter, Bill didn't know who Andrea Balosky was. Now she is someone he will never forget. Andrea, also known as Andrea Leong Scaddon (maiden name) and Nyima Llamo (Buddhist name), had been making quilts off and on (mostly off, according to her) since 1964. Born and raised in Oahu, Hawaii, Andrea was on the cutting edge of the art quilt movement in the 1980s and 1990s while living in Washington State. Her book, *Transitions: Unblocking the Creative Quilter Within* (Martingale and Co., Inc., 1996) is still held in high regard, and many art quilters consider the book a must-read classic. Twelve years after its publication, praise for the book continues to show up on blogs and e-mail messages on list serves touting how it caused a turning point in quilt artists' creative lives. Besides Quilt National, Andrea's work had been shown in many celebrated venues, including the Sisters Outdoor Quilt Show; International Quilt Festival in Houston, Texas; Vision 2000 in Vienna, Austria; and the White House.

Andrea has led an interesting and varied life. She served as a Peace Corps volunteer in Malaysia and the Solomon Islands (Guadalcanal). She participated in a United Nations meeting held in Katmandu in 1977. In March 2004, Andrea left the United States for Darjeeling, India, to begin a nine-month Tibetan language program. As a practitioner of Tibetan Buddhism, it was her hope to become more proficient in reading religious books with her language studies. To help finance her trip, Andrea held a weekend sale in Sisters of many of her possessions, which attracted a large number of friends and well-wishers. "I am a fiercely independent woman, but it was very nice to have so many wonderful friends help, particularly the women who helped package my quilting materials and move my goods from Camp Sherman to Sisters for the sale," she said at the time. She left behind her few remaining worldly possessions and all of her quilts at her home in Camp Sherman, Oregon. At the pinnacle of a successful quilt career, she left it all behind. Her ninth-month stay in India turned into a permanent residency.

As the saying goes, "Curiosity killed the cat, but satisfaction brought her back." Bill could not contain himself. "Do you mind if I ask you something?" he said. She faced him and nodded for him to go ahead. "How do you get from point A to point B? In other words, what was your path from the world of quilting to Buddhism?" She replied, "Do you have time?"

She shared about the time when her father was dying in the hospital, hooked up to many different machines. It was a heartbreaking experience. To her, it seemed like an unfair and undignified way to leave the world. Before he died, she promised him that she would find a better path for her life. It so happened that around that time she discovered a book about Buddhism, and it changed her life.

After finishing her story, she thanked Bill for giving her quilt a good home. *Night Flight* was made in 1982 while she was living in Seattle, Washington. In 1983 (Quilt National only happens every other year and always on the odd years), 350 artists submitted 766 works to be considered for inclusion in the show. *Night Flight* was one of seventy-nine quilts by seventy-two artists accepted. The show that year was also the first Quilt National to travel. Included in Quilt National's publication on the show, *The Quilt: New Directions for American Tradition* (Schiffer Publishing, January 1984), *Night Flight* was an important work in Andrea's life. She considered it her first masterpiece. For her, giving it away was a true test of her faith.

> *Night Flight was an important work in Andrea's life. She considered it her first masterpiece. For her, giving it away was a true test of her faith.*

The 62-inch by 69-inch wall hanging is machine pieced and hand quilted. It is constructed entirely of commercial fabrics. The quilting stitches are tiny and even with machinelike perfection. The back is one piece of indigo/navy fabric with a small white floral print. This fabric was also used for the binding. The quilt label sewn onto the back has fine lines created in hand embroidery that says "Andrea Scadden '82"—the artist's maiden name and the year she made the quilt. In her artist's statement, she shares, "In *Night Flight* I hoped to capture the feeling of dramatic motion as inspired by the thousands of Canadian geese that in late autumn launch themselves at daybreak from Nebraska ponds in their southern migration."

Serendipity was certainly at play at the Sisters Outdoor Quilt Show that warm, sunny day in July 2010. In 1989, Bill had bought his first antique quilt. He originally started collecting quilts to display as wall art in his home. After he had the first quilt, he realized he could not safely display it year-round, so he bought a second quilt, which led to the purchase of more and more quilts. When he would purchase a new piece of furniture or redecorate, he'd get a new quilt to go with the décor. He moved around a lot and changed interior décor a lot, so he ended up with "a pile of quilts." His quilt collection now contains more than eighty quilts, mostly made before 1900.

After many years of collecting, Bill decided to focus on collecting quilts of a rare and highly difficult classical pieced quilt pattern called Rocky Mountain Road (or New York Beauty). In 1930, Mountain Mist published a pattern called New York Beauty, based on the earlier pattern most commonly called Rocky Mountain Road. From that point forward, the world has known this pattern primarily as New York Beauty. Bill currently owns twenty examples, the oldest dating between 1810 and 1829 and the majority from the 1850s to the 1890s.

Andrea's quilt is completely different from Bill's other quilts. Most of his quilts were made by quiltmakers that are now deceased and are not well known. Andrea's quilt is the only quilt in his collection that was made in his lifetime and the only quilt accompanied by a story about meeting the maker in person. It is also the only example he has from the late twentieth century art quilt movement and the only one that could be called a pictorial quilt. "It's so completely outside the box for me. I love that about it," Bill shares.

Bill considers all of his quilts to be works of art and has displayed them on his walls for more than twenty years. Until recently, his quilts were simply a rotating private collection. As the number of his quilts grew, he thought more and more about cultural outreach and sharing his collection with the general public. He now does presentations and shares his quilts with groups throughout Oregon. Since starting the Oregon Quilt Project in 2010 with Martha Spark, his presentations have evolved, and each quilt is now a talking point about the importance of preserving quilt history in Oregon.

Andrea's quilt is a welcomed addition and offers a unique storytelling opportunity. Bill will hang the quilt in his home at some point, but probably for only a few months so that it remains in good condition. He wants the quilt to stay in the Pacific Northwest, most likely as part of a museum collection, something he promised Andrea that he would make happen. The experience has made him open to collecting more art quilts, and he even has his eye on one.

Andrea had yet another gift to give during that visit to the Sisters Quilt Show, so she presented *Jerry's Garden* (part of her 1995 Gaia Mandala II, Mandala Series) to the Oregon Quilt Project to use as a raffle quilt for a fundraiser. *Jerry's Garden*, part of Andrea's prolific creative period, is made of Shoo Fly and Churn Dash blocks, 40½ inches by 40½ inches. It is all about her former husband and his frustrations with having a garden in Oregon. She had not mentioned this quilt when she first arrived at the booth and probably happened upon it when she was searching her stored belongs for the quilt to give Bill. The gift of this quilt seemed to be easier for her. Bill also hopes this quilt stays in the Pacific Northwest when it finds a new owner. Andrea gladly filled out the Oregon Quilt Project questionnaire so both quilts have now been documented for the project.

As Andrea was getting ready to leave, Bill wanted to know, "Will I ever see you again?" Andrea took his hand and said, "In another life. In another life." Bill replied, "I hope our paths cross again in *this* life." They hugged, and she quickly disappeared into the crowd.

Bill has spent time reflecting on the whole experience and the gift. It is not every day that two historical and masterpiece quilts are given to a perfect stranger. Bill has asked himself, "Why me? What did I do to deserve such good fortune, this supreme act of generosity?" Bill has concluded that the true gift was not so much the material object but what it represents. The gift was the experience of meeting an incredible person, hearing her story, and, for just a few moments, glimpsing her peaceful, amazing world.

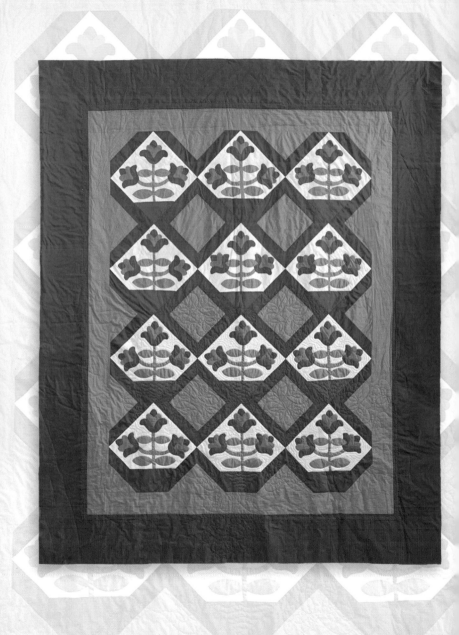

# THE OLDEST UFO

The large front porch of the one-and-a-half story dark green maritime home with white trim had always been full of the most amazing geraniums that you can imagine. Bessie Thompson used to paint pictures of them and had a journal in which she dutifully recorded the bloom of each plant. She was still painting them at 102 when she was in a nursing home.

The Thompsons came from strong stock. Bessie's mother, Martha, was widowed in 1895 after her husband, Robert, drowned in the town well. He left her with five children to raise (one daughter would later die in the influenza epidemic), which she managed by taking in washing and selling needlework. She lived her entire life in this family home in St. Andrews, New Brunswick, Canada. People remember her as a very domineering and strong-willed woman, but then again, she probably had to be given the circumstances. Bessie and her

*Tulip*
Made by Martha Thompson (blocks), St. Andrews, New Brunswick, Canada,
   and Heather Lair, Gimli, Manitoba, Canada
1920s to the present
78 x 90 inches
Cotton/polyester blend, machine pieced, hand appliquéd, and hand quilted
*Collection of Heather Lair, photo by Heather Lair*

sister, Gladys, lived with their mother and never married. They both became teachers. Bessie was very artistic and would have gone to art school had she been allowed, but such things did not happen in those days. There were also stories of an engagement ring for Bessie at one point, but the details have now been lost. Both Bessie and Gladys made beautiful embroidered pieces, clothes, knitted items, and crocheted lace, but they did not make quilts, at least not that anyone knows.

According to Bessie, Martha made quilts until the late 1920s. She was forced to quit when her eyesight failed. None of her quilts survived. Martha died in the late 1960s at age one hundred. Gladys died in 1984, and Bessie lived in the home until 1990, when she moved into a nursing home. The family members were all "savers," though they might be called "hoarders" today. It took many years to go through and clean out the family home. Unfortunately, the women's frugality also extended to everyday household repairs—they just did not happen, which meant this once-impressive home would have to be torn down by the new owners.

During the cleaning-out process, though, family member Shirley MacNeish discovered a large envelope that contained some cardboard templates; enough appliqué shapes in pinks, blues, and greens cut out to make ten blocks; and a little bit of extra white fabric. Since her cousin, Heather Lair, was the only quiltmaker in the family, Shirley decided it was fitting that she pass the contents of the envelope on to her. Martha Thompson's son, Glenn, was Heather's grandfather.

After puzzling over the appliqué shapes, Heather, a fairly new quiltmaker at the time, realized that the only pattern that made sense was a complicated tulip shape. Her first step was to recreate the pattern by making new cardboard templates, then carefully tracing around each template with a pencil on the fabric pieces to create an accurate line for stitching the pieces to the background. This was Heather's first attempt at appliqué, and now when she teaches appliqué, she shows her students how unskilled she was then. She feels that sharing her less-than-perfect work (you can see her stitches) is important for her students. Everyone has to begin somewhere, and, as with any new skill, it takes practice to become good at it.

Heather appliquéd the blocks not having a clue how the quilt was originally designed to look. She also added two blocks to make twelve. If you look closely at the quilt, you will see a difference in the background white and the other fabrics added for these two blocks. Since Heather did not have access to 100 percent cotton fabric in the color that she needed at the time, the blue is a cotton/polyester blend. She did her best to match the colors as closely as she could. Martha had not left any clues for the quilt, and Bessie had no recollection of the project. Heather's inspiration for setting the blocks on point came from a beautiful quilt she saw in *Quilter's Newsletter Magazine* by a quiltmaker from Germany. (Bonnie Leman founded *Quilter's Newsletter Magazine* in 1969—the first, and for many years the *only*, magazine devoted solely to the interests of quiltmakers.)

The quilt, which was machine pieced, ended up being 78 inches by 90 inches and could be used on a double bed. Years later, Heather came across the book *Quilts and Other Bed Coverings in the Canadian Tradition* by Ruth McKendry

Martha Thompson's hometown of St. Andrews.

(Discovery Books, 1979) and discovered within it the quilt her great-grandmother intended to make. The books says, "Conventional Tulip: quilt, appliquéd, cotton, mauve, yellow and white; Egor Family, Kingston, Frontenac County; 1st quarter century, W. 170 cm, 202 cm (67, 80 in.). The tulip design is quilted in the alternate blocks." This information from the book did, indeed, confirm the timeline and probably the quilt that her great-grandmother had begun to make.

Heather finds it interesting that Martha was making current patterns of the time. Women farther away from the populated areas of the United States and Canada generally followed quilt patterns that were at least ten years old. St. Andrews, a small town in New Brunswick near the border with Maine, was an active fishing community and tourist destination at the time, but it was not an urban center on the forefront of popular trends. Heather's aunts and great-grandmother did travel often to Boston to visit family and purchase shoes and clothing, however, so perhaps Martha picked up the pattern on a trip to Boston. Or the pattern may have been on some batting or some other kind of household packaging. Quilt patterns could be found even on soap packages at that time. It is unlikely that she purchased the pattern because the family had to be very frugal, but Heather's aunts often sent away for free patterns from magazines (many were found while cleaning out the house).

While Heather laid out the quilt "wrong," she does feel it still has some charm. The original quilt had two borders while Heather's has a small inner sashing and a large blue border. The quilting in the alternate blocks is also different. However, she feels the design of the quilt's blocks is still as fresh and modern today as it was in the 1920s.

In 1985, Heather took some of extra white poplin fabric in the original package and used it in another quilt. It was a quilt that her family used often, so it got a lot of washing. Unfortunately, the white poplin fabric that is the base for the appliqué in Martha's quilt has completely disintegrated. Heather wishes she had tested the fabric before she attempted to appliqué the blocks in Martha's quilt. She believes that the quilt might have been left unfinished because it was waiting for some better base fabric. To replace the fabric now would mean completely dismantling the quilt—something that Heather would never do at this stage—but this also means that upon completion it can never be used on a bed. No one will ever be able to sleep under it. The quilt will simply be a display piece and family heirloom.

> *She feels the design of the quilt's blocks is still as fresh and modern today as it was in the 1920s.*

Throughout her life, Heather has studied and taught a variety of styles, uses of color, and techniques used by quiltmakers and needleworkers throughout the world. Though she first developed a passion for traditional quilts, for many years now, Heather has been using these traditional techniques to make art and landscape quilts. All of her work is hand quilted and hand appliquéd, and each piece is individually designed. Many of her quilts can be seen in television shows and in movies (*Maneater, Stone Angel, Chilled in Miami,* and *Make It Happen,* to name a few). Her quilts grace the walls and beds of homes and public buildings from Manitoba to Japan, Iceland, and South Africa. Despite all this, her great-grandmother's quilt remains one of her prized possessions.

Heather did not begin hand quilting Martha's quilt until the 1990s, and she still takes it out every once in a while to work on it. The blue cotton/polyester fabric added to the quilting challenge because it is not an easy fabric to hand quilt. She does intend to finish it, although she has been tempted to leave it unfinished so that it could be passed to yet another generation. "I enjoy the bragging rights I get from having an eighty-five-year-old UFO [unfinished object]!" ✎

# ELIZABETH

With each of the many moves the Bartelsmeyer family would undertake (central Illinois to Nashville, Illinois, to Belleville, Illinois, and back home again to Nashville), the quilt would travel in a box simply labeled "old quilt." At each destination, the box would be shoved into the farthest corner of the attic—never discarded, never mentioned, and never loved, for sixty years.

In the summer of 1996, after Marjorie Elizabeth Shirley Bartelsmeyer died, her son, Karl, and daughter-in-law, Sandy, began the task of cleaning out her home. Late one hot day, Karl emerged from the dusty attic carrying a battered box labeled "old quilt." Sandy immediately remembered the day when Marjorie had mentioned an old quilt. The conversation had taken place in 1994, after Marjorie's great-granddaughter Brianna Elizabeth Bartelsmeyer (Karl and Sandy's own granddaughter) was born and Sandy was visiting. Out of the blue, Marjorie said, "Brianna should get that old quilt because

---

**Carolina Lily**
Made by Nancy Elizabeth Martin Shirley, Illinois
Circa 1850–1860
59½ x 82 inches
Cotton; hand appliquéd, hand pieced, and hand quilted
*Collection of Sandy Bartelsmeyer, photo by Bernie Weithorn*

her middle name is Elizabeth." Sandy asked, "What are you talking about?" Marjorie explained how she had come to inherit the quilt years after her grandmother had died. "It's in a box in the attic, but I haven't looked at it since I got it in the 1930s when Aunt Pru gave it to me. I just kept taking it with me every move that I made." Sandy offered to look for it right there and then, but Marjorie said, "No, just leave it be. It's ugly. Brianna can have it when I pass on." No more was said about it and life went on.

When it came time to open the box, Sandy and Karl truly thought that they would find some old, worn patchwork quilt in shades of black and brown. How exciting it was to discover a beautiful Carolina Lily quilt in Turkey red, dark green, cheddar, and white instead. However, the quilt reeked! The smell was absolutely horrible, and the fabrics in the quilt had yellowed. Sandy took it home and promptly put the quilt in the washing machine, thinking that it would be okay if it were cleaned in cold water, on the delicate cycle, with Woolite. After removing it from the washing machine, she hung it outside to dry in the sun. Fortunately, it survived and came out smelling fine. Now Sandy wanted to know the entire story of the quilt.

The Civil War would not begin for five more years. On December 15, 1856, at the age of fourteen, Nancy Elizabeth Martin would walk down the aisle. She married William Jefferson Shirley in the southern Illinois town of Nashville. William was twenty-one. Nancy had been born in Bluford County, Tennessee, but her family moved to Nashville early in her childhood. William had been born in Illinois after his parents moved to the area from Virginia. Many of the people living in southern Illinois were former Southerners who had moved there when the government opened up public land for purchase.

William could not read or write when they married, but Nancy patiently taught him. They owned a farm in Ashley, Illinois, and raised seven children. In 1916, they celebrated their sixtieth wedding anniversary. Nancy died on October 14, 1917, and William followed her on May 23, 1920. Nancy was known as a prolific quiltmaker and made quilts her entire life.

Atha Prudence "Prudie" was the second-to-the-last child born to Nancy and William, in 1878. Prudie never married, but, like many unmarried women, became a schoolteacher. (In those days, only unmarried women were allowed to be teachers, married women were actually ineligible.) She lived with her parents until the death of her father, then died herself in 1939.

Prudie's favorite niece was her younger brother's daughter, Marjorie. Marjorie had always lived close, and she was also a teacher like Prudie. Marjorie attended McKendree College in Lebanon, Illinois (a Methodist college and the oldest college in Illinois), as did a farm boy named Ralph Bartelsmeyer, who was two years older. They knew each other from high school, but started dating seriously during college. On Good Friday of 1929, they went to Missouri and got married.

Ralph planned to go to the University of Illinois in Champaign to study civil engineering in the fall of 1929. They thought they would announce their marriage in the summer of 1929, and Marjorie would go with him to Champaign and finish her college education there. However, in the spring of

1929, Ralph told his parents he was "thinking" about getting married. His father's reaction was, "In that case, you can stay home and farm. You don't need to go off to college." Ralph had no intention of becoming a farmer, and Marjorie did not want to be a farmer's wife. They decided to keep their marriage a secret until Ralph finished college. The only person who knew they were married was Marjorie's mother, Lura. Lura did not even tell her husband because she said, "He can't ever keep a secret." Marjorie returned to McKendree College in the fall, and Ralph transferred to the University of Illinois as planned.

In the spring of 1930, Marjorie finished her two-year degree in vocal music performance. She went home to live with her parents. That fall, she was hired as a first-grade teacher. Marjorie had no background in teaching and came home after the first day in tears. Somehow, Aunt Pru was notified (probably by mail), and the first weekend after the start of school, she took the train to Nashville and brought with her all sorts of teaching aids and worksheets and gave Marjorie a few teaching pointers as well. Marjorie's students that year in the first grade included one fourteen-year-old boy who was taller than her and another "semi-disturbed" young man who refused to put an "i" in his name (David) because he said that the dot on the eye was looking at him. At the end of the year, Marjorie promoted them both because she could not face teaching them again the next

> *They decided to keep their marriage a secret until Ralph finished college.*

year. At the close of the school year, she was informed that the next year she would be teaching second grade. Fortunately, Ralph had graduated.

During the Great Depression, married men were given priority in hiring for jobs, so Ralph included that fact on his application with the Illinois Division of Highways. Unfortunately, he also put his parents' address on the application. His mother found out about the marriage when she opened an envelope addressed to "Mr. and Mrs. Bartelsmeyer." It was a job offer telling Ralph that he and his wife were to report for employment. To say his mother was upset would be putting it mildly, but eventually it all worked out.

Marjorie and Ralph spent several years traveling from job to job for the Illinois Division of Highways until they settled back in Nashville before their first child was born in 1936. Karl was born in 1941. Shortly after they moved back to Nashville, Aunt Pru gave Marjorie one of her mother's quilts. Aunt Pru explained to her that she was getting the quilt because her middle name was Elizabeth just like her grandmother's. It was impressed upon Marjorie that the quilt had been important to Marjorie's grandmother because it was thought to be her grandmother's wedding quilt, so it should be treasured.

Marjorie's daughter-in-law, Sandy, sewed in high school and college, making clothing and crafts. After she gave birth to her third son, however, she gave up sewing entirely. In 1983, she married Karl, who was a widower with three sons. They raised their children together.

From 1980 until 1999, when their youngest graduated, they had children in college. It wasn't until Sandy turned fifty in 1999 that she took up quiltmaking. A friend was teaching a class at a local quilt shop on a Piece O' Cake Designs wall hanging, and Sandy thought it would be fun to make one. At the time, she did not own a sewing machine or even a piece of fabric. She now owns three sewing machines and a room full of fabric. She hand quilts all of her quilts except for those for her seven grandchildren, which she did by machine. Through her studies, she has learned how lucky she was when she washed Marjorie's quilt and now understands how to preserve quilts. It is now stored in an acid-free box.

A couple of years ago, when their home was on the holiday home tour, Sandy took Marjorie's quilt out of storage to display it on her bed. "It looked beautiful. I also had a friend stationed next to it the entire time of the tour to make sure no one touched it." The quilt has been appraised twice—once in 1999 and then again in 2005. The appraisals have confirmed that the time when the quilt was made was circa 1850–1860. The backing is muslin and the fabrics are all cotton. The 59½x82-inch quilt has very good overall hand quilting and the stitches are even. It is in good condition considering the age and how it was stored.

Brianna is excited about receiving the gift when she gets a little older (she's only sixteen). "Until that time, this grandma is keeping it safe," says Sandy. ✍

# CRAZY ALL THIS TIME

The crazy quilt was carefully folded and placed in the trunk where it would stay for 121 years. The quilt, always stored in that trunk, would travel from Maine to Massachusetts to Connecticut before returning to Maine. Susan "Susie" Fogarty will never know that her quilt has brought her distinction at her alma mater, but her great-nephew thinks she would be pleased. The colorful, highly embroidered silk and velvet quilt features delicate flowers, a cat, horseshoes, birds, a large salmon, a heart, and even a picture of Susie with dark hair, bangs and a long braid drawn on a doily. "Class of '89" is stitched with white thread over a maroon background and is by far the largest feature on the quilt. A neatly embroidered yellow F on black velvet, presumably for Fogarty, and a red A on gray silk, which stands for someone or something we will never know, can also be found. The quilt, with its tan backing, is in remarkably good condition.

---

**Crazy quilt**
Maker unknown, possibly Susan "Susie" Fogarty, Waterville, Maine
1889
54 x 51 inches
Silk and velvet; hand pieced and embroidered
Donated to Waterville High School by John Tracy, Susie's great nephew.
*Photographed by Dennis Griggs*

Historians credit the Japanese exhibit in the 1876 Philadelphia Centennial Exposition for inspiring the crazy quilt with its asymmetrical art. This type of quilt became quite a fad during the 1880s in the United States. Japan had been open to the West for less than twenty years at that time, and the mysteries of the country and its arts fascinated Americans. Crazy quilts differ from "regular" quilts because the careful geometric design of a quilt block was much less important in crazy quilts, so the makers were able to employ much smaller and more irregularly shaped pieces of fabric. In comparison to standard quilts, crazy quilts were far more likely to have exotic and expensive pieces of fabric, such as velvet, silk, satin, and taffeta. Also incorporated into the quilts were buttons, lace, ribbons, beads, paint, printed silk bands that were used to tie bundles of cigars together, commemorative handkerchiefs, and other exotic materials.

Also popular during Victorian times were Stevengraphs, small pictures made of woven silk resembling elaborate illuminated ribbons or pictorial bookmarks. Makers of crazy quilts would often incorporate these into their quilts.

Crazy quilts could be assembled in three different ways: in squares, like a block-style quilt; in strips; or as a single layer of cloth. Whatever the construction method, the maker usually turned under the edges of the different fabrics and sewed them together by hand with embroidery stitches. Crazy quilts were not made to sleep under, but as showpieces. They were used as throws on chairs and couches and even as table decorations. They were often exhibited in the parlor, where visitors could admire them.

Many crazy quilts served as the textile scrapbooks of the day and provided great opportunities for self-expression and individual creativity. Objects embroidered onto crazy quilts had meaning. Some, like the horseshoe, were pretty universal and stood for luck; roses were symbols of love; a pansy represented remembrance. The large salmon found on Susie Fogarty's quilt probably represents the fishing industry in Waterville, Maine. It was an important source of revenue for the town starting in the late 1700s, with salmon, shad, and alewives shipped primarily to markets in Boston. Susie loved cats her entire life, so it is not surprising to find one on the quilt.

We will never know for sure whether Susie made the quilt or the quilt was made for her. From her great-nephew, John Tracy, we do know that Susie's mother would not have allowed the quilt to be put on display. "It's just how our family was. You just didn't share those kinds of things," John explains.

Many families originally came to the Waterville area to find work in the textile and paper mills that once thrived along the banks of the mighty Kennebec River. Located in Kennebec County, Waterville is fifty-two miles south of Bangor and eighty miles north of Portland. Waterville became a town in 1802. In 1883, Waterville was large enough to become a city, but didn't accept that elevated status until 1888. Susie's parents, John and Susan Fogarty, had emigrated from Ireland and were among the oldest families in town. John's brother had come with them, but he left for the West Coast and was never heard from again.

The class of 1889 at Waterville Senior High School had only five students (all girls—Susie, Emma Knauff, Mertie Mayo, Winifred Roundy, and Mary Tarbell) and was only the thirteenth graduating class for the school. All the boys in town were attending the Coburn Classical Institute, a boys-only high school, because their families could afford the tuition. Another explanation for the lack of boys in the graduating class is that in 1888 a "full quota" of Waterville men responded to the governor's call for the Spanish-American War. The Coburn Classical Institute building burned in 1955. Waterville Senior High School is now the only high school in Kennebec County.

Susie lived her entire life in a little white house with a large lilac bush close to the street at 266 Main Street in Waterville. The house was long ago torn down and replaced by a brick office building. The youngest child and only daughter of John and Susan, Susie was born on November 20, 1870 in Maine. After graduating from high school, she taught school for a few years, then clerked at Spaulding's Book Store before becoming a saleswoman and buyer for Wardwell's Dry Goods Store. A few years before her retirement in 1932, she was employed at Blake's Hardware Store. Her domineering mother probably did not make any suitors feel welcome, so Susie never married, nor did her brother William "Willie." Susan "wore the pants in the family" and was an accomplished sewer who also made quilts. Two patchwork quilts, one intricately pieced and the other quite worn, were also found in the trunk. They were probably

> *Susie lived her entire life in a little white house with a large lilac bush close to the street at 266 Main Street in Waterville.*

made by Susie's mother. Susie took care of her mother until her death in 1916 at the age of eighty-six, and William until he died in 1932 at the age of sixty-seven.

Susie loved music and had a beautiful voice. For many years, she was a member of the Sacred Heart Church choir and the Cecilia Choral Society. She was an active member of the Waterville Woman's Club and was passionate about her community and Maine. Rachel Carson's summer house was in nearby Southport, and Rachel profoundly influenced Susie and the way she lived her life. Susie was known for her friendliness and enthusiasm.

Thomas Fogarty, one of Susie's brothers, stopped for a visit on his way to taking his grandson, John Tracy, to college at the University of Maine in Orono. During the visit, Thomas became ill, so the sixty-five-mile trip to John's college became Susie's responsibility. This trip would cement their relationship. Afterward, John would spend every Thanksgiving and occasional weekends with his great-aunt. One of their favorite activities was listening to Susie's extensive collection of early 1900s music on her crank Victrola. John, who had grown up in Lexington, Massachusetts, did not see his great-aunt after his college graduation. The attack on Pearl Harbor caused him to enlist in the Army, as most of his male classmates did, to fight in World War II.

Susie died suddenly on April 1, 1949. She had been seriously ill a few months before, but appeared to be recovering, so her friends were "greatly surprised." John was twenty-nine years old at the time. Susie left many things in her estate to him: He received the trunk, the Victrola, and her record collection, as well as many of the family's miscellaneous belongings that had meaning to Susie. When John received the trunk, it was the first time he saw the contents. Not once in all his visits had he seen the quilts.

John worked for Southern New England Telephone Company in New Haven, Connecticut, and he and his wife had five daughters. None of them were ever interested in family history or took up quiltmaking. One of John's daughters took the pristine and more precisely made of the two patchwork quilts off with her to college to use as a decoration in her dorm room. During her stay at college, much to John's regret, the quilt somehow disappeared. Even now there is a part of him that still cannot forgive her. He truly wishes he had that quilt, too.

Over the years, John would occasionally remove the crazy quilt from the trunk and admire it. It brought back good memories for him. After his wife died and he turned ninety years old, he decided it was time to find a new home for the quilt. He offered the quilt to each of his daughters, and they all declined to take it, so he decided that if Susie's high school would take the quilt, he would give it to them.

As office manager and secretary, Claudia Pellerin gets lots of calls at Waterville Senior High School, but this one took her breath away. A man was calling to ask if the school would like a quilt made 121 years ago in Waterville, a quilt that seemed to be a memento of his great aunt's graduating class, the class of 1889. Without missing a beat, Claudia replied, "Absolutely." Claudia is in awe that John took the time to call the school and offer it as a gift. "I think it's just so nice that he thought of us," she says. "Most people wouldn't bother." Principal Don Reiter, who majored in history and is a former history teacher, is excited to have an artifact from the early history of the institution to display at the school. The plan is to have the quilt framed and hung in the new media center/library.

"Believe me, Susie was a very dedicated person to both Maine and to Waterville. I think she would be happy to know that her quilt was now with her high school," shares John Tracy. Everyone involved believes that the quilt has been shut away far too long. Now it is time for it to be out in the world for all to see so the students, parents, teachers, and staff at Waterville Senior High School now have a piece of their early history. 🖎

# A QUILT IN THREE PIECES

**A**merica! *Life will be better in America. Happiness will be found.* Katie Friedman believed that with all her heart. Staying in Czaklo, Slovakia, was out of the question. After her father's death, her mother, Leibe, had married quickly, fearing that she would not be able to provide for her three children. Katie had experienced cruelty from her stepbrothers, who loved to tie her to one side of a water-turn wheel, with a mule on the other side, and laughingly force her to walk around and around for hours. Staying also meant enduring tough economic times and living in a world that was rampantly anti-Semitic. Leibe agreed with Katie and found the money to pay for her passage to the United States. So in 1885, at age twelve, Katie made her first attempt to board the ship for the New World.

*Reiter Quilt*
Album quilt
Artist unidentified; probably Baltimore, Maryland
Circa 1848–1850
101 x 101 inches
Cotton and wool
This quilt is now part of the collection of the American Folk Art Museum,
    New York (2002.2.1), a gift of Katherine Amelia Wine in honor of her grandmother,
    Theresa Reiter Gross, and the makers of the quilt: her great-grandmother,
    Katie Friedman Reiter, and her great-great-grandmother, Liebe Gross Friedman.
*Photo by John Parnell*

"No unaccompanied child allowed! Off with you!" said the man at the gangplank. Not to be deterred, she patiently waited for an opportunity. When she spotted a family with many children, she simply attached herself to them and quietly boarded unnoticed.

In the hustle and bustle of Ellis Island, Katie was met by her uncle Jacob, who came down to "the boat" regularly, looking for friends and relatives. She went to work in his grocery store in Newark, New Jersey. When she was seventeen, she married Benjamin Reiter, and they moved more than 350 miles away to the steel town of McKeesport, Pennsylvania. Reasonably comfortable financially, Katie was able to send for her mother, her sister Amelia, and her brother Ephraim in 1899. However, her happiness was broken when her firstborn son, Adolph, died of "the flux" (or dysentery) later that same year. (In the nineteenth century, four out of ten children died before the age of six.) More heartache was to come when, shortly thereafter, Ephraim drowned while boating on the Youghiogheny River near McKeesport.

Soon after the deaths, Katie and Leibe began working on a quilt. Although they were Orthodox Jews, the Reiters had assimilated into the general McKeesport community and had access to fairs where quilts were shown and related periodicals and guides were available. Katie may also have been exposed to the bold and brightly colored album quilts made in the vicinity of Newark, a city with a strong German community.

The colorful cotton and wool quilt begun by the two women was quite large, measuring 101 inches by 101 inches. It had sixteen embellished pictorial blocks on a white cotton background. The border had undulating vines interspersed with floral sprays. Most of the blocks were variations of floral motifs, and many of the appliquéd pieces were embellished with embroidery, which outlined the pieces or provided details. The fabrics were solid red, yellow, orange, and green, with only a few printed pieces. Black, a color rarely used in appliqué quilts of the time, appeared in five places: as part of three animals and two human figures. Many of the colored appliquéd pieces were heavily padded, creating a dimensional effect. The American eagle, heavily symbolic to immigrant families, was placed prominently in one square. The family also feels that the two equestrian figures in black represent the two deceased children. *Reiter* means "rider" in German and refers to an Austrian ancestor of Benjamin's who returned a hero from the Franco-Prussian war.

Katie had seven more children, the youngest of whom was her daughter Tess. Tess then had a daughter herself, Leba, who was named after her grandmother. Leba remembers when her parents took her in 1930, at the age of four, to what she thought was a visit with her grandmother. It was actually a tonsillectomy. When she returned from the doctor's office, she was put to bed in what seemed, in her semi-etherized state, to be "a garden of earthly delights." She remembers waking the morning after and discovering that she was recuperating under her grandmother's exquisite quilt.

Later that year, Tess gave birth to Leba's brother, Benjamin. Katie was delighted with the new baby, and especially one named after her husband. No one knows why she completely removed the border from her quilt and used six blocks to make a crib quilt for little "Benjy," leaving the quilt in three pieces, but she did.

In 1942, upon Katie's death at age sixty-nine, the quilt passed to Tess, where it would remain in three pieces, tucked safely away in a closet for the next forty years. In 1973, Leba's husband, David, died of a sudden heart attack at forty-seven, leaving Leba with a broken heart and four children to raise on her own. Within two years, she moved from Tucson, Arizona, to Tiburon, California, hoping new horizons would lighten her gloom. In 1976, while waiting to learn whether she had passed the bar exam, she took a six-week course on quiltmaking at a local college. Leba became thoroughly enamored with the Nine Patch potholder she made during the class. She wanted to make more quilts, so she called her mother and said, "Let's make a quilt!"

History was not to repeat itself, however. Tess replied, "No." But, she said, "Since you're so interested in quilts, I'll send you Grandma's quilt, and you can find someone to put it back together." *Sounds like a great project*, Leba thought. The quilt arrived a week later.

Having only a vague recollection of it from her childhood, Leba now believed that it was the most beautiful quilt ever made. She realized that she did not have the skills to put it back together, so off to the telephone directory she headed. When she called the Quilt Connection (a store that sold mostly antique quilts) in San Rafael, she connected with one of the owners, Julie Silber. Julie made arrangements for the quilt to be put back together. She also informed Leba that very few older quilts were made by Jewish women, and she asked if it could be included in the exhibition *American Quilts: A Handmade Legacy*, which she was curating for the Oakland Museum. "Yes!" replied Leba.

The Oakland Museum show resulted in many invitations to display the quilt around the country. Leba always insisted on being the one to transport it, for it was far too important to her to risk any possibility of loss or damage. Finally, the touring ended, and the quilt was once again wrapped in a white sheet and placed at the back of a closet. This time it was in Leba's closet, where it would rest until 1997.

While Leba was watching *Antiques Roadshow* on PBS, she saw that someone had brought in a Baltimore Album quilt to be appraised. It looked a little like her family's quilt, although not as big or as beautiful. Leba could not believe it was appraised at $75,000. The next day, she raced to the phone to call Julie, who confirmed the value of the quilt would be approximately the same. *Oh my!* thought Leba, *The quilt had not even been on my list of things to save if the house caught on fire.*

This knowledge changed everything. Leba called all her cousins, but only one remembered the quilt. Then she called her children. They were all grown, with cats, dogs, and children of their own. The quilt would not be safe with them. Selling the quilt was tempting but unsettling. She really didn't want anyone else to own it. After another consultation with Julie, now the curator for the Esprit Quilt Collection, she decided to donate the quilt to a museum, a task that turned out to be more difficult than anyone imagined.

Leba's first attempt at donation was to a museum in California. While the museum expressed interest, no one ever called her back. Julie put her in touch with Joel Kopp, an art collector. He made recommendations, too. The second museum contacted also expressed interest, and again no one called back. A third suggestion was rejected by Leba. Finally, Leba contacted the American Folk Art Museum in New York City. Joel shared that the museum was a good choice because its fabric storage was superb and it seldom deacquisitioned (sold) its art. Leba did not know at that time that in 1979, several trustees came together to purchase the famous *Bird of Paradise* quilt top for the museum. This acquisition represented a turning point: the art of quiltmaking would become a major emphasis in the collection and programs of the museum.

When Leba called the museum, she was put through to Stacy Hollander, Senior Curator/Director of Exhibitions. Stacy replied to the offer by stating she would have to see the quilt before making any commitments, and asked for Leba's name. Leba told her and explained that she was named after her great-grandmother, adding, "The quilt is named after my grandmother. It is the *Reiter Quilt*."

"The *Reiter Quilt*? You want to give us the *Reiter Quilt*?" Stacy had admired it at several exhibitions where it had been on display. "Wait a minute."

Minutes later, Leba was speaking to the director of the museum, George Wertkin, who said, "Of course we want the quilt." All the arrangements were made there and then.

The American Folk Art Museum treated Leba like royalty. A photograph of the quilt and an announcement of the new acquisition were published in the *New York Times*. The quilt was featured on the cover of an issue of the museum's quarterly magazine, accompanied by a long article on its provenance. Leba decided to donate the quilt in the name of her daughter, Katherine Amelia Wine, who was named after her great-grandmother, Katie Reiter, and Katie's sister Amelia. In return for the gift, lifetime memberships to the museum were given to Leba, her children, and her cousins.

Leba has waited for donor's remorse, but to date still thinks she did the right thing. The quilt's third resurrection inspired her to write a novel based on stories of five generations of mothers in her family, written as the biography of a family quilt. The book is called *Stitches in Time* (Many Names Press, 2006).

As with most families, it is more the norm than not for family histories to evolve over time and for some facts to become further romanticized. Continuing research on quilts, however, broadens our knowledge and understanding of these wonderful artifacts. This is true for the *Reiter Quilt*. Based upon new research conducted on Baltimore Album quilts by Ronda McAllen, the museum now believes that the quilt belongs to the mid-nineteenth century (c.1848–1850) Baltimore Album quilts. The *Reiter Quilt* seems to relate closely to a quilt (c. 1850) possibly made by Mrs. Josiah Goodman in the collection of the Maryland Historical Society in Baltimore. While there is no doubt that the quilt was passed down through members of the Reiter family, it is unknown how it originally came into the family's hands. It is known that there was a long association of this quilt in the Reiter family and that it was made by Jewish quiltmakers, cut up, and reassembled. There is also no doubt that this quilt, regardless of the makers, has had a huge impact on the Reiter family and will be a lasting legacy for all of us. ᴎ

# A FRENCH BED

Janine Jannière had never been interested in antiques. She had never expressed any interest in the needlework in her family. She was not a collector, not even as a child. And yet, the desire to experience something new and the look of an antiques store in an old colonial home would create the path that would change quilt history.

Having lived in Paris, Janine wanted to experience a new environment while she studied English. She loved American culture, particularly that of nineteenth-century rural America, so instead of studying in New York or San Francisco, she chose the University of Connecticut in Storrs. While driving through the Connecticut countryside, Janine stopped at an antiques stored called What's It Shop to explore the inside of the wonderful old colonial home that housed it. The shop owner, Clare, was busy sewing and simply told her to look around.

---

**Bed with patchwork hangings and bedcover**
Artist unknown, southern France
Circa 1830 for the textiles, earlier for the bed
Height of the headboard, 60 inches
Textiles are all pieced work of printed cottons and French toiles using the English paper
    template method; no quilting.
*Photographed by Yohann Deslandes, Musées Départementaux, for the exhibition in Château
de Martainville, Musée des Traditions et Arts Normands, 2003. Now in the collection of the
Musée National des Arts et Traditions Populaires.*

When Janine traveled to the second floor, she encountered a "thing" on the wall that shocked her like nothing before. It was love at first sight. Janine talks about the experience: "This is like a painting. This is so incredible. I think what really touched me was the warmth. There was life coming out of it for me. I was really moved. It was not only something intellectual where you see something and you admire how it is made, it was almost something physical. I immediately wanted to touch it."

Quickly making her way down the stairs, she asked, "Is the thing on the wall for sale?" Clare told her it was. "What is it?" Clare explained, using the quilt she was working on as an example. "You cut up fabric, then sew it back together? I've never heard of such a thing," said Janine. Opening drawers, Clare showed her even more quilts. "It was like a little child when you open gifts under the Christmas tree, and you see something for the first time. I really had never seen anything like it," says Janine.

The quilt was reserved for a friend of Clare's in Vermont. Janine had to wait six months until the friend finally decided she did not want to purchase it before she would be united with her first love—a simple, richly colored silk Log Cabin quilt with a brown border made during Victorian times. It was the beginning of a lifelong passion for quilts.

It was 1975, and though quilts were inexpensive at the time, Janine was a student without much money. She couldn't buy as many as she desired, but when she did, she bought without being selective. She became good friends with Clare, who would come to call her "my French granddaughter." Clare even made Janine a quilt.

Clare's whole life revolved around making quilts. Originally from Kentucky, she shared stories of her grandmother's, mother's, and aunt's quiltmaking. Janine wanted to understand why this object was so important. Was it the same for other women? Was this just a particular story of this family, or were there others? She quickly decided that she wanted to get a Ph.D., and she would study women and quilts.

On the European continent, people generally agree that the European tour of the Jonathan Holstein and Gail van der Hoof quilt collection, which began at Les Arts Décoratifs in Paris in 1972, triggered the ensuing quilt boom. However, and for whatever reason, the museum and research worlds in France were not interested in investigating French patchwork. They simply believed it was not a French tradition.

When Janine returned to France, there were many challenges to overcome. There is no word for "quilt" in French. The word *patchwork* is used in France, but not to describe an object. *Patchwork* refers to a patchwork of people, a patchwork of ideas. Her first challenge was how to describe what she wanted to study and how to gain acceptance for it. One adviser said, "You want to do a Ph.D. on a bedcover?"

"I was really looked down upon," says Janine. After much searching, she found a progressive group within the American Studies department at the University of Paris VIII that finally accepted her proposal. Her first step was to read all that she could on quilts, and a book by Jonathan Holstein was particularly inspiring.

In 1984, Janine returned to the United States. She had received a grant from the Fulbright Commission to travel around West Virginia, Tennessee, and Kentucky to find quiltmakers who were not involved with the Quilt Revival. Instead, she wanted to meet and talk with quiltmakers who were still making quilts like their mothers and grandmothers so she could compare them with quilts made by people involved in the Quilt Revival.

Her first stop was in New York to meet with Jonathan Holstein, who suggested she connect with Shelly Zegart. Jonathan was working with Shelly and the Kentucky Quilt Project to document Kentucky quilts. Meeting Shelly in Louisville, Kentucky, would change Janine's life. Shelly immediately put Janine in touch with quiltmakers in Appalachia, then introduced her to a contemporary quilt artist in Ohio and many others who were part of the Quilt Revival so that Janine could compare the significance of quilts in the lives of traditional quiltmakers to contemporary quiltmakers, then to the quiltmakers of the Quilt Revival. Shelly also took Janine to the International Quilt Festival in Houston, Texas.

*She had never seen anything like this bed with its quilt and curtains in the United States.*

"I think the genius of American women is that they used the old European techniques and transformed them, and there was this sense of freedom that was not in the orderly British quilts," says Janine. "They transformed everything, that's why it's a sign of your culture and your history in the nineteenth century. You didn't invent the technique, but you transformed it, simplified it, and made it really vibrant and really free."

Since Janine's focus was on American quilts and her profession was teaching English, she knew nothing of quiltmaking or textiles within France. In 1985, she began lecturing on American quilts in France. One day, she got a call from someone saying, "We have this antiques dealer who has a quilt in her antiques shop, and she doesn't know what it is but would like to estimate it. I'm not an appraiser, but I'm sure I can tell her what it is."

Janine asked, "What is it?"

"It's a Grandmother's Flower Garden," said the caller. At first Janine thought, *There are dozens of American Grandmother's Flower Garden quilts from the 1930s, and they all look alike.* She was not particularly interested, but since she is curious by nature, she asked more questions.

"There are figures on the fabric. Oh, and I forgot to tell you, it's a bed and there's a cover and then there's a crown. And then there are curtains."

"Oh, wow!" Janine said. "I'm coming!"

She drove the thirty miles to the shop, and it was amazing. She had never seen anything like this bed with its quilt and curtains in the United States, and she did not think anything like it existed in England, but she was uncertain. Her intuition told her that it was French because of the themes she could see in the fabric, but she felt she could be wrong. Taking copious notes and photographs, she e-mailed them to Jonathan Holstein, who promised her that he would tell her what he thought in forty-eight hours. He later called her and said, "Buy it!"

"I can't. I don't have any money," said Janine.

"Let me talk to Shelly," Jonathan replied. A deal was struck that Jonathan and Shelly would purchase the bed with its quilt and curtains, and Janine would study it.

Janine spent five years conducting her research. Her travels took her to the different archives in the main textile institutions in France in her attempt to identify the different fabrics. There she searched through boxes filled with samples and file cards. The toile fabrics were easy to identify because they were large, but the tiny little hexagons with the herd of sheep or a dog were much more difficult. Thirty-three pictorial toiles representing twenty-seven separate designs (some toiles were used in different colors) were identified. They roughly cover the period 1795–1830. Out of these, nineteen are from Oberkampf's factory in Jouy-en-Josas (representing fourteen designs in different colors) and designed mainly by its most famous artist, Jean-Baptiste Huet.

Resistance came in many forms. One curator said, "It's not because all the fabrics are from France that makes this French." Janine understood her point, but felt the symbols emphasized that it was French. "There were the kings in France, Louis the Sixteenth and Louis the Fifteenth, represented in the fabrics."

After identifying that all the fabrics were indeed French, she set out to find the family. She knew the bed was too elaborate to be from a modest family, and toile was expensive in the nineteenth century. After searching for two years, she found an antiques dealer, Albin Abelanet, in the western Pyrenees, in southwestern France near the Spanish border. He had purchased the bed from a family who lived in a castle in a remote area near the village of Cassagnes. Albin had actually slept in the bed! He told her about the family. He was also pleased that she was doing the research because he had never had the time.

Janine visited the local and regional archives to find out all she could about the family. She discovered that the themes found in the patchwork fit exactly the history of the family—the fact that they had a vast wine domain, that they raised sheep and sold the wool, that they were royalists who left France, that the family crest included a hound, and that they had been extremely religious. Everything fit.

When Janine arrived at the twelfth-century castle, her heart beat quickly with anticipation. The castle was in a very remote area and had originally served as a fortress on the ancient border of France. It was part of an estate that had been owned by the same family since 1700. The descendents had kept no records of the textile set. However, Janine did discover where and how the bed was made, and she found that it was typical for the area. The origin of the bed's shape can be found in the district of Olot, a town in Catulonia, which from the seventeenth century onward produced very characteristic beds known as *Olotinas* in Spanish. The bed (1790–1810) was made of rosewood, fruitwood, and pear wood with brass and bronze mounts. The crown above the bed is spruce with copper posts. The height of the headboard is 60 inches. The two bed curtains each measure 88½ by 33½ inches.

Now Janine knew that women were making patchwork in France at one time, but she needed to find proof. She thought she might find it in women's magazines. When Janine met with a curator of costumes who had studied women's magazines, she informed Janine that she had not seen any patchwork patterns, but Janine wanted to see this for herself. She knew the bed was made around 1820, and she knew that quilt patterns were mostly published after that date. So when Janine looked through the archives, she looked after 1850. To her delight, she found patterns that covered a full page. She even discovered them in an 1862 article that stated, "Mosaic patchwork is a technique that came to us from England." Here was the proof! Jonathan and Shelly agreed.

Through quilt guilds and friends, "almost like a miracle," she was led to other quilts. She found one with Napoleon in the center from Marseilles. She found another one in a castle in Montpellier and continued to find more. These discoveries would lead to the exhibition *Mosaiques d'étoffes: à la recherch de l'hexagone* (*Mosaic Patchwork: In Search of the Hexagon*) at the Musée des Traditions et Arts Normands (a regional folk art museum) in Martainville near Rouen from May to October in 2003 (with its accompanying catalog). The exhibition included forty-one quilts.

The bed was acquired by the Musée National des Arts et Traditions Populaires (the French National Folk Art Museum), which has a great research center for anthropology and French folk art traditions. The museum, which will be called Musée des Civilisations de l'Europe et de la Méditerranée (Museum of European and Mediterranean Civilizations), will move from Paris to Marseille, opening in 2013 when Marseille becomes one of the European Union's cultural capitals of Europe for the year. Since the bed is a result of mixed influences and exchanges of several European traditions it is a much-welcomed addition to the museum's collection.

"I am just one little person. Imagine if we had thousands of people looking for quilts," says Janine. 🐚

**Log Cabin quilt, Barn Raising design**
Artist unknown, Connecticut
Date unknown
57x57 inches
Silk and velvet
*Collection of Janine Jannière, photo by Olivier Languillon*

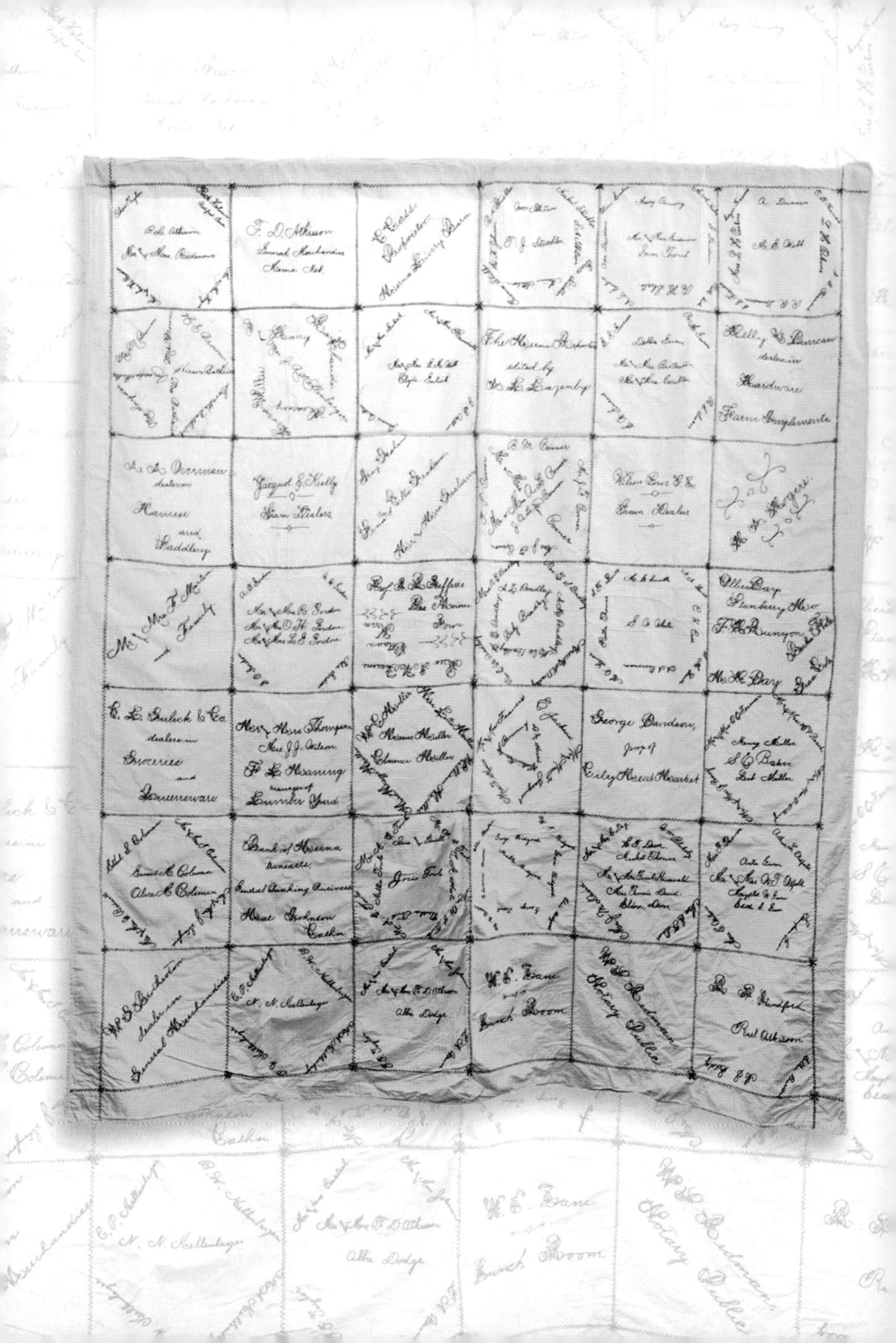
F. D. Atkinson
General Merchandise
The Havana Reporter
edited by
Kelly & Duncan
dealer in
Hardware
Farm Implements
dealer in
Harness
and
Saddlery
Grain Dealers
Grain Dealer
C. L. Gulick & Co
dealer in
Groceries
and
Queensware
George Davidson
City Meat Market
Lumber Yard
Bank of Havana
W. E. Bane
Lunch Room
Notary Public
General Merchandise

# HISTORY RETURNED

The Roadrunners, as this group of four friends from Watseka, Illinois, liked to call themselves, loved to take road trips together several times a year in search of American-made baskets and antiques. They did so for nearly thirty years until health and age began to prevent them. Their travels took them to shops and museums around Illinois, Indiana, Ohio, Kentucky, and Tennessee. When they began, their trips only took a day, but over the years, they grew to seven to eight days. Arline Crowley remained a member even when she had moved to Princeton, Illinois.

The group looked mainly for baskets, which meant that they quickly exhausted their sources in Illinois. During one of their trips, in a store located in a barn where everything had a layer of dirt, Arline came across a quilt filled with signatures. "I can picture that barn so clearly, but I just can't remember where it was," says Arline. The quilt was thrown over the top

---

**Signature quilt**
Ladies Aid Society of the Methodist Prosestant Church, Merna, Nebraska
1892
72 x 82 inches
Cotton; tacked, with 230 embroidered signatures
Donated to the Merna Public Library by Arline Crowley
*Photo by Deb Hostick*

of a chair that was full of "junk." The quilt was clean so she suspected it had just been placed there, and she felt a strong need to rescue it. "It just looked too important to just leave there to get dirty."

Arline's sister was a quiltmaker and belonged to a group at their church. Arline had always admired quilts even though she did not collect them. She did know these kinds of quilts had been made for special occasions. Arline cannot remember how much she paid for the quilt, but she does know it was $35 to $65 because her rule was to never pay more than $65 for anything, and she suspects it was closer to $35. She never really looked at the quilt much after the day she bought it, just an occasional glance in the box where she kept it and then only at the few visible blocks.

"I had heard people say that when they got older, they started giving things away. I just thought that was nuts until I turned seventy-two, and now I understand," Arline says. The quilt was stored away for more than twenty years until she decided it was time to do something about it and noticed, upon careful inspection, that one square listed "Atkisson, General Merchandise, Merna" and included the stitched abbreviation "Neb." It was then she knew that she might have a chance of finding someone in Merna who would want it.

An Internet search brought up the Nebraska community of Merna and the Brenizer Library's telephone number. The fact that she happened to call on one of the three afternoons a week that the library is open was fortuitous. Arline reached the library's director, Vickie Burnett, who was having a crazy day. Children were lined up waiting to share their artwork and receive refreshments. Volunteer Dee Adams was painting the library's walls. Arline asked if there might be a group that would be interested in researching the history and the story about the events surrounding the quilt's creation. She was also hopeful that some relatives whose signatures were carefully stitched on the quilt's blocks might still be living in the area. Vickie almost could not contain her excitement as she frantically took notes from the call. A piece of history was going to be returned to Custer County.

The quilt arrived a few days later. Merna historian and Custer County Historical Society president Dee Adams began researching the origin and travels of this unique record of the village's past. Dee had time to dedicate to research since retiring from the U.S. Postal Service after working there for thirty-three years. She felt her years working for the post office made her good at spotting names while conducting research.

Nebraska became the thirty-sixth state in 1864. The first settlers arrived in the Merna area (central Nebraska) in 1878. Two years later, there was a post office and a population of thirty people. By 1890, the town was booming with a school, hotels, cafes, general stores, a meat market, livery stables, a flour mill, grain elevators, a wagon maker, a dressmaker, a drugstore, and churches. The population had grown to more than 200 people. Today the population is less than 400.

In late 1891, A. L. Lazenby began circulating a newspaper called the *Merna Reporter*, which had a subscription rate of $1 a year but would be short-lived. While it was published, however, it seems nothing in town escaped the watchful eye of this press. In April 28, 1892, the paper reported: "The Ladies

Aid Society has decided to pay the church debt of the M.P. [Methodist Protestant] Church, and will make a block quilt. On each block will be the business of every business man who advertises in this medium. The blocks are only 90 cents and any one can afford to take one. After the quilt is finished, it will be sold at auction." Some of the *Merna Reporter* editions are missing, so the answers to the questions of when or if an auction occurred, who ultimately took possession, and how much the quilt raised are for now unanswered.

The history of the newspaper and how its issues became available for research on the quilt is a discovery story of its own. According to S. D. Butcher's *Pioneer History of Custer County, and Short Sketches of Early Days in Nebraska* (The Merchants Publishing Co., 1901), after the closing of the *Merna Reporter* under Lazenby, "It was resurrected in 1893 by Captain [Prince Albert] Gatchell and continued until the fall of 1894, when he moved it to Sheridan, Wyoming, continuing in the newspaper business there until his appointment as register of the land office in that state. In 1899 Rev. Clifton commenced the publication of the *Merna Sun* which, in the spring of 1900 he sold to Theo. A. Miller, who abandoned the paper in January of the present year, and returned to his home in Omaha. Most of the material was shipped back to York, from whence it had been leased." In July 1999, the Nebraska State Historical Society in Lincoln received a donation of 127 issues (from 1891 to 1894) from Sunny Irvine Taylor of Kaycee, Wyoming. Sunny found the newspapers in old fake leather bags while cleaning out a shed that had belonged to Arnold and Alicia Gatchell Lund, relatives of her husband. Alicia's father was Captain Gatchell (1841–1925).

There are 230 carefully embroidered names in crimson thread on white fabric listed on the 72-inch by 82-inch quilt. There are fourteen blocks dedicated to Merna businesses and twenty-eight more blocks that list entire families or groups of individuals. The Bradley family block even has "Baby Bradley," perhaps an unborn child, embroidered in the middle of the block and surrounded by family names. The stitches look as if they were sewn yesterday, and only a few stains can be found on the quilt. The stitching of the signatures appears to have all been done by one person who embellished the first letter of the names in her own style. It has no batting and the quilt is tied—each block is tacked at the corners, so there is no actual quilting.

*It seems nothing in town escaped the watchful eye of the* Merna Reporter.

It only took a few minutes to determine the approximate date the quilt was made because of the block that read, "The *Merna Reporter* Edited by A. L. Lazenby." Another block near the center listed "Prof. A. R. Jeffries Des Moines Iowa" and "Rev. J. M. Frame Ottawa Kan." Thanks to the newspaper, at least part of the quilt's story has been pieced together: "Evangelist Frame and Prof. Jeffries of Des Moines, Iowa, arrived on last Saturday evening and will hold a three or four weeks series of revivals. Prof. Jeffries is a good singer and it will pay any one well to hear him sing. The services are held at the M.P. Church. Song Service commencing promptly at 7:30 p.m. and services at 8:00" (*Merna Reporter*, March 3, 1892).

"Rev. J. M. Frame and Prof. Jeffries closed their five weeks series of meetings here on last Sunday night. During their stay here they have succeeded in drawing a crowded house every night rain or shine, and have the means of bringing about seventy-five persons into the church at this place. They left the first of the week for their next point of holding meetings, at Ottawa, Kansas. While we regret to see these gentlemen leave Merna, we hope that the good that they have done will live for many years" (*Merna Reporter*, April 7, 1892).

"The Ladies Aid Society of the M.P. Church met at the church on Friday afternoon. Some changes were made in the officers. Mrs. O. H. Gordon was elected president, Mrs. B. L. Atkisson, secretary, and Mrs. Day, treasurer. The ladies are engaged in an album quilt. Will meet at the church every Friday afternoon at 2:30. Every lady interested in the church welfare is invited and expected to come" (*Merna Reporter*, April 21, 1892).

The newspaper's mention of the quilt stops here. One guess might be that the album blocks and the business blocks were joined due to less-than-expected interest from the local merchants. Since the average number of names on each quilt block is about nine, we can speculate that the families and individuals might have paid ten cents for each name on the block (making each block cost the same 90 cents charged to the businesses for their blocks). This would have made an estimated $37.80 raised for the Ladies Aid Society through the selling of space for names.

The original church still stands at the corner of Thomas Street and Castile Avenue, but the original members would not recognize the remodeled building. Other changes have occurred over time. The Methodist Protestant Church voted to transfer to the United Brethren Church in 1904. In 1968, the United Brethren Church and the Methodist Church joined to become the United Methodist Church.

At the July Heritage Day celebration in the summer of 2010, many visitors stopped by the library to view the quilt. The list of local residents who can identify their ancestors' names is growing. Many of their grandchildren still live in the area. Dee Adams is asking each family to write a short biography on their family or have her interview them so a biography can be written.

The Brenizer Public Library was designed in Prairie School style and was built in 1916. It is listed on the National Register of Historical Places and is in the process of renovation and restoration. A special place to preserve and display the quilt has been added to the list of ongoing projects.

Dee admits that unraveling the history of the quilt has become an obsession. "I can't stop researching," she says. She hopes to continue looking until all of the mysteries are solved. Arline is just happy to have been able to give back a little early history to a community. "It was never about the items I bought when we were out on the road. It was about the great friends, the camaraderie, the memories, and the pie. We did love finding places with great pie." 🍃

# A LOCKED DOOR
# CHANGES EVERYTHING

I n the spring of 1999, too much coffee, a locked door, an
open closet, and a quilt top dramatically changed the life of
a quiltmaker from Gee's Bend, Alabama.

In the late 1930s, as part of the New Deal programs during
President Roosevelt's administration, the government bought
the former Pettway plantation in Gee's Bend. Gee's Bend, also
known as Boykin, began as a cotton plantation in the early
1800s and was named after its owner, Joseph Gee, the first
white man to settle in the area. It was an isolated community,
surrounded on three sides by the Alabama River and linked to
the outside world by a single road, which was unpaved until the
late 1960s. It is located about thirty miles southwest of Selma.

**Housetop variation**
Made by Mary Lee Bendolph and pieced and quilted by Essie Bendolph Pettway,
    Gee's Bend, Alabama
1998
72 x 76 inches
Cotton corduroy, twill, and assorted polyesters; hand pieced and hand quilted
An image of this quilt appeared on a 39-cent U.S. postage stamp in 2006.
*Collection of Tinwood Media, photo by Steve Pitkin/Pitkin Studio*

In 1845, the Gee family sold the plantation to a relative, Mark Pettway, to settle a $29,000 debt. After the Civil War, the formerly enslaved residents, a majority of which share the name Pettway, remained as tenant farmers and developed their own distinctive local culture. As part of Roosevelt's "New Deal," a project began to return the land to the residents and families that had worked it since the days of slavery. Families were able to buy land with no-interest or low-interest loans from the government. Each family was assisted with the building of a house. With each house came a few acres around the homestead and room for a garden, a barn, a smokehouse, and a few additional outbuildings. They also had roughly one hundred acres of land in the "bottoms," the best land for cotton planting, and twenty acres in the "piney woods," from which the families could get their timber for additional building or repair. Over the years, those houses generally stayed in the family. As parents died, their homes generally went to their children, who continued to raise their families in those houses.

Mary Lee Bendolph's home had originally been built for the Bendolph family. Her husband, Rubin, was raised in the house. When Mary Lee and Rubin married in 1955, they moved into the house and raised their eight children in it, seven boys and one daughter.

Many owners of "Roosevelt" houses added on to these homes to accommodate their growing families. Over the years, kitchens were enlarged, plumbing was moved indoors, and rooms were amended or added as resources became available. What had started as a two-bedroom house with a common room and a kitchen area often became something very different. And usually these additions were added as needed and did not follow any architectural plans.

Mary Lee's house was one of those houses. In the last few decades, her family had added two bathrooms, built several bedrooms, enclosed the porch, and made many other changes that radically altered the way the house looked and the flow of traffic within the house. It was this strange architectural plan that led to the discovery of a quilt that changed the lives of both Mary Lee and Matt Arnett.

Gee's Bend became an important part of the mid-1960s Freedom Quilting Bee, an offshoot of the Civil Rights movement designed to boost family income and foster community development by selling handcrafts to outsiders. Mary Lee was part of the Freedom Quilting Bee, but quit because she did not feel the pay was fair. Gee's Bend and the area around the community had been known for its quilts for decades before Matt Arnett and his father, Bill, made their first trip there in 1997, scouting for quilts. They did not expect to find much there, given the number of people who had been to the area before them, many looking for quilts. What they found would come as a great surprise to them and would also later surprise the world.

During the first trips Matt made to Gee's Bend with his dad, often accompanied by their friend Mary McCarthy, lodging was an issue. There were not any hotels close to Gee's Bend. One of their early trips coincided with the big family reunion weekend in the area, and hotels in Camden (the county seat located across the river from Gee's Bend) and in Selma (the largest town in the area, located in Dallas County) were all booked. Cell phone coverage in the area was spotty, at best, and this was in the days before the readily available PDAs and cell phone applications that make such things easier to find. Matt and Bill had driven late into the night before finally finding accommodations in the town of Thomasville.

When Mary Lee learned that they had stayed so far away, she opened her house to them, saying, "My mama always welcomed people into our house and taught me to never turn people away." She continued by saying that if they ever needed a place to stay, they could stay with her. Since everyone in the community knew her and where she lived, it would also be a great way for people in the community to find them.

Mary Lee is known as the "memory keeper." As word spread around Gee's Bend about the two men who were interviewing quiltmakers and buying quilts, the requests for them to visit people's homes grew. Mary Lee was receiving a lot of those calls. It made sense to her for them to stay with her, making it easier for them to connect with people in the community. She also informed them that word had spread about "two white men who must be crazy because they were overpaying for ugly and raggly quilts." They accepted her very generous offer for a place to stay. They offered to pay her what they'd pay for a hotel, but she refused their offer. Bill and Matt would visit with her often.

Making quilts was considered a domestic responsibility for women in this area, with many learning from their mothers. Mary Lee was no exception. However, unlike some of the other quiltmakers, she had very few quilts in her possession by the time the Arnetts met her. In Gee's Bend, quilts were used until they were worn out, then thrown away or recycled in many interesting and unusual ways: Quilts were taken apart and usable parts recycled into other quilts; quilts were torn and used for domestic purposes such as rags, mops, diapers, trivets, etc; quilts were put into pots and lit on fire to create billows of smoke to keep mosquitoes away. But even though quilts were considered practical, they were also used as gifts to mark special occasions, such as graduations, marriages, or birthdays.

During one of his stays, Matt excused himself to use the bathroom. A door on his usual path had been locked, so Matt had to use an alternate route, which meant detouring through another room. It was there that a flash of color caught his eye. In a makeshift closet on top of carefully folded blankets, Matt saw what he thought was a corner of a quilt. The Housetop-variation quilt had been made in 1998 after Mary Lee's sister-in-law, who had moved to Bridgeport, Connecticut, had sent her some double-knit leisure suits with instructions to give them away. "Clothes from way back yonder, don't nobody wear no more, and the pants was all bell-bottom," Mary Lee said, "we ain't that out of style here. I was going to take them to the Salvation Army but didn't have no way to get there, so I just made quilts out of them." She had added some cotton and corduroy fabrics to the assorted polyesters to make the pink, red, white, brown, and black quilt. It had remained on the shelf unfinished because Mary Lee truly believed it was unattractive. Matt knew otherwise.

As he opened it, he told Mary Lee that it was one of the most beautiful works of art he'd ever laid his eyes on.

She laughed out loud and said, "That ugly thing?"

"Yes," he gushed. "Why didn't you ever show this to us?"

"I didn't think you'd be interested in *that.*"

"This is exactly the kind of thing we are interested in."

"Well, if you want it, take it."

"No, no, no. We want to buy it."

"You want to pay money for *that*? Well let me and Essie [her daughter] quilt it, then you can take it."

As the Arnetts were organizing *The Quilts of Gee's Bend* exhibition and book, the quilt was selected for inclusion. It turned out to be the only Mary Lee Bendolph quilt selected for the first exhibition, which opened in Houston, Texas, in 2001. As the exhibition toured and the women accompanied the show around the country, Mary Lee emerged as the leading spokesperson for the community. The quilt was shown in many museums and featured in many newspaper and magazine reviews of the exhibition. Mary Lee appeared on numerous television shows, including *CBS Sunday Morning*, *PBS NewsHour* with Jim Lehrer, and *The Oprah Winfrey Show*, among many others. Mary Lee also made fine art prints with Paulson Bott Press in Berkeley, California, which were displayed in United States embassies around the world.

Early in 2004, Derry Noyes, art director with the U.S. Postal Service, spotted the Gee's Bend quilts in a catalog from the Corcoran Gallery of Art and brought the images to the Stamp Advisory Committee. On August 24, 2006, the U.S. Postal Service issued the *Quilts of Gee's Bend* commemorative postage stamps at the American Philatelic Society's annual convention and philatelic exhibition in Rosemont, Illinois. The quilts became the sixth group to be featured in the American Treasures Series, intended to showcase beautiful works of American fine art and crafts. The ten quilts on these stamps were created between 1940 and 2001, and among them was

Mary Lee's Housetop quilt. After Mary Anne Gibbons, senior vice president and general counsel for the U.S. Postal Service, revealed the stamps, Mary Lee said, "This is such an honor. I just have to give praise to the Lord. We all are blessed to have our quilts on a postage stamp. We never had any idea this would happen to us. We are all so honored." And then she started to sing a gospel song.

Mary Lee Bendolph's quilts and etchings have now been shown in dozens of museums across the United States. Her quilt, an untitled Housetop-variation quilt that Matt Arnett found hidden as a quilt top, was just the beginning of the success for Mary Lee and for the quiltmakers of Gee's Bend that would soon follow. Certainly the quilt would have eventually surfaced, but it is doubtful that it would have surfaced in time to be included in the groundbreaking exhibition that caught the world by surprise.

Mary Lee has continued to make quilts, and her work was featured in the second major Gee's Bend traveling exhibition and book, *Gee's Bend: The Architecture of the Quilt*. Her work also formed the basis for the exhibition and book *Mary Lee Bendolph, Gee's Bend Quilts, and Beyond*, which premiered at the Austin Museum of Art in 2006. The exhibition finished traveling in late 2009, but a series of her smaller quilts continues to travel.

Unfortunately, Mary Lee suffered a stroke a week after returning from the Obama inauguration in 2009, so she is traveling less. However, making quilts still remains a part of her life. She also continues to help those who are less fortunate than her—one of the joys she often expresses when sharing stories about her success. ॐ

# MOONLIGHT MAGIC

L ife was not easy for those who lived through the tumultuous times of the Great Depression and World War II. Warm, dry weather was a trademark of the early 1930s in Ohio and much of the United States. Dry soil and parched vegetation provided little water for evaporation, so surfaces heated to temperatures not normally experienced in the Heartland, making life even harder. Many who survived would never forget those years of "waste not, want not," even when their lives got easier. While quiltmaking was very much a part of the back-to-basics movement of the Depression era, many women on farms had been making quilts their entire lives.

John William "Billy" and Sarah Elizabeth "Lizzie" Guyton owned a farm in Hardin County, in northwestern Ohio. They had three sons. The youngest was eleven when their daughter, Leah Gladys, was born, named after Lizzie's mother, Leah

---

*Fish and Baskets*
Made by Sarah Elizabeth "Lizzie" Guyton and Leah Grubb Hetrick (top) and Leah Gladys
   Guyton Stump (quilting)
Circa 1860–1870 (top), 1980s (quilting)
67 x 67 inches
Cotton; hand pieced and hand quilted
*Collection of Dawn Goldsmith, photo by Dawn Goldsmith*

Grubb Hetrick. Lizzie was forty-two at the time. Like so many other farmers during the Depression, their family lost their beloved farm to the "Insurance Company," which held the papers on it.

During the Depression, Lizzie was known to the hobos and travelers throughout the area for her pies and generosity. As farm people, they ate well, being able to grow most of their own food. Mother and daughter got along pretty well, but they disagreed about pies. Leah made deep-dish pies, and Lizzie would complain that she couldn't take a bite without getting her nose in it—shallow pies were her forte. They were both, however, excellent pie bakers and quiltmakers.

Lizzie died in 1958 at the age of ninety-two. Likely because she needed to care for her mother, Leah didn't marry until 1944, when she was thirty-one years old, to Benjamin Franklin Stump. She was forty when she gave birth to Dawn, her only child. Much to Dawn's regret, she did not inherit the gift of being able to make great pies. However, she did make quilts.

In 1985, when the family's hot-water heater sprang a leak, soaking the boxes stored nearby, Leah salvaged what she could, including an old, partially finished quilt top. It was one of several projects that she had inherited from her mother. After laundering the top, she decided it was worth completing. She added a border with some brown fabric that she had on hand, then quickly quilted it by hand and finished it.

Since Leah had come of age during the Depression, she liked to make quilt patterns that were popular in those times—Grandmother's Flower Garden, Double Wedding Ring, Lone Star, or Bethlehem Star. Most of the quilts that she made after

Dawn was born were never completed; however, together with Dawn, she did make two Log Cabin Quilt-in-a-Day quilts for her grandsons' beds. She hand quilted them in the ditch and quickly vowed that she would never to do that again! As a member of the Town and Country Quilters in the 1980s and 1990s, she liked to try new patterns and would make them for exchanges with this group.

It was in the early 1980s when Dawn, her husband, Derrol Goldsmith, and their two sons, David and Nick, moved back to Dawn's hometown of LaFayette, Ohio. They had purchased a 150-year-old clapboard house that was in sad repair with lots of drafts. They were in the process of rehabbing it when Dawn was given this salvaged brown quilt. "It's not perfect, that's for sure, but it's useful," Leah told her, thinking it could be used to wrap up in while sitting on the couch or given to her two grandsons, who liked to curl up in afghans and blankets while lying on the floor watching television. However, Dawn decided to hang the quilt on a newly refinished wall, a feat accomplished to the accompaniment of low-level grumbling from her husband: "It's a blanket. It belongs on a bed." All grumbling ceased once they stepped back and admired the new artwork on the wall. They felt a sense of family came from the old hand-stitched quilt.

The 67-inch-square quilt of cotton fabric was hand pieced into a basket pattern. Each basket block was a 10-inch square made from scraps left over from clothing. It hangs a little crooked, which just added to the charm. One basket had been turned sideways making it look like a fish, so Dawn's sons christened it the *Fish and Baskets* quilt.

For the Goldsmith family, the skewed block was an endearment that gave the quilt personality. However, when Leah came to visit, she did not share their opinion. She was embarrassed at the lack of perfection, especially when it came to her hand quilting. "My stitches aren't even," she pointed out, adding, "I can't believe you hung that on the wall." However, a gift is a gift. The quilt was Dawn's to do with as she wished, and she wished for the quilt to hang on the wall.

A year passed. The family faced bouts of unemployment and a crushing stack of bills. One night, after several frustrated squabbles, Dawn was restless and unable to sleep. She slipped quietly out of bed and tiptoed downstairs in search of some relief. Food had become her choice for comfort, so she headed to the kitchen and the refrigerator, which meant a trip through the family room. As Dawn passed through the room, moonlight swept in through the window and landed on the quilt. As she glanced at the now-familiar wall hanging, she stopped dead in her tracks, rubbed her eyes, and looked again. Caught in the eerie moonlight was an aberration. It could not be the same quilt. In its place, there was a quilt with a geometric design of Grecian urns and triangles. Not a basket in sight. The antique fabrics held their new images for a while, but then slowly slipped back into their traditional roles, baskets once again.

*As Dawn glanced at the now-familiar wall hanging, she stopped dead in her tracks.*

Running quickly up the stairs, she roused her sleeping husband and two sons, forcibly marching them down the stairs to witness the midnight revelation. Sleep-filled eyes finally focused on the quilt, and together they watched as the moonlight and fabrics did their magic.

"Well, I'll be."

"You see it, too?"

"I see it, Mom! The fish is gone!"

"Wait. It *is* there. Just look again."

They ignored the call of the new day and stood together before the quilt, its illusion transforming them from a knot of angry individuals into a family once again. For Dawn, it was a sign. If a quilt could change by moonlight, they could change a few financial woes and things would get better. After all, the women in her family had faced their own difficulties, and she could do no less.

The quilt no longer hangs in Dawn's home. It has gotten too worn and fragile, so now it is safely tucked away. Dawn herself does not have much to show for her own quiltmaking efforts. Mostly, she sewed clothes for her family, sewed curtains for the house, wrote stories and magazine articles, was on staff at the local newspapers, and wrote about people who were doing exciting things that included quilting. She made her first full-sized quilt in the 1980s and helped her mother with the quilts for her sons. She maintains the highly popular blog *Subversive Stitchers: Women Armed with Needles*. She dabbles in a few quilt projects these days, but mostly she cheers on other fabric artists. Dawn's mother, now ninety-eight years old, still frowns when the *Fish and Baskets* quilt is mentioned.

Dawn had always believed that the quilt top had been made by her grandmother, Lizzie. However, during a recent conversation with her mother, it was revealed that the quilt was not made by Dawn's grandmother, but by her great-grandmother, Leah, sometime between 1860 and 1870. While this news came as a big surprise, for Dawn it only strengthens the bond she feels for the quilt. And whenever something seems impossible, all Dawn has to do is look at the quilt, feel the generations of strong women from her family gather around her, and know that nothing is impossible.

*Note:* The idea that quiltmakers intentionally placed a block incorrectly to create a "humility block" (because only God is perfect) has been researched extensively. Research has shown that the "humility block" seems to be a figment of mid-twentieth-century imagination, another story to romanticize the past. For the June 1988 issue of *Quilter's Newsletter Magazine*, quilt historian Barbara Brackman tried to trace the story back to its origins. She said she could find no mention of the practice in any of the early twentieth-century quilt books.

People often cite that the practice originated with Amish quiltmakers. When quilt historian and American Quilter's Society certified quilt appraiser Bobbie Aug spent time with an Old Order Amish family in Lancaster, Pennsylvania, she asked them about the humility block. To them, "Only God was perfect and to imply that a quilt could be perfectly made and, therefore, had to have an intentional mistake in order to bring good luck, etc., would be blasphemy." The story is similar to one told about intentional mistakes being made while creating Oriental rugs. (Most rug historians also consider the story of this practice to be fiction.) Most quiltmakers know that mistakes happen easily without intentionally making them happen. In all likelihood, the skewed basket block was probably a simple mistake and might have been the reason that the top went unfinished. It was simply waiting for the time and inclination to fix it, which never happened. &

# ONE WORD

I t is rare for an "ordinary," working-class woman to shed new light on our perceptions of the past. As Melissa Woodson walked through the vast quilt collection at the International Quilt Study Center and Museum (IQSC) in 2001, she was not thinking about making a great discovery. She was simply looking for a quilt to study as a project for her textile analysis class at the University of Nebraska–Lincoln. Quilt No. 1997.007.0852, with the single word notation "genealogy," caught her attention. Since her father was an avid genealogist, she was intrigued, and she knew if she needed help, she could rely on him. This quilt, a friendship quilt, had thirty-six signatures of women long dead. She thought she could use the names to guide her as she tried to uncover the quilt's history and origins.

Melissa decided to try to obtain information about the quilt from the New York and Connecticut dealers who had

---

**Signature quilt**
Made by Mercy Jane Bancroft Blair, South Apalachin, New York
Circa 1855–1863
90 x 79 inches
Cotton; hand pieced and hand quilted
*Courtesy of the Ardis and Robert James Collection, International Quilt Study Center and Museum, University of Nebraska–Lincoln (1997.007.0852)*

sold it before it was donated to the IQSC. Working backward through the dealers, she was hoping that one of them would know something, but not one did.

A handwritten note pinned to the quilt provided a clue: "This quilt was made by ladies of South Apalachin for Aunt Jane Blair, sister of Achsa Bancroft Moe, mother of Lucy Moe Wood, mother of Roy Wood." Despite the note, the quilt's uniform design and careful block placement suggested a single quiltmaker.

Melissa began her research by analyzing the one hundred cotton and woolen fabrics in the quilt. Figuring out the time bracket for when the quilt was made would be vital in tracing the names. From the analysis, she was able to determine that the fabrics were from 1845 to 1865. These dates were also consistent with the friendship block pattern used in the quilt.

Unfortunately, many of the quilt's inked signatures were faded and unreadable, which presented yet another challenge. Melissa began by photographing the signatures using a digital camera. Since light damages fabric, the photography had to be accomplished without using flash. Using photo enhancement software, she electronically manipulated the images until she could read all the names.

Printing the signature images on transparencies and overlaying them, she could compare the handwriting on the different blocks. It did not take long to establish that the handwriting on all the blocks was created by the same person, most likely the person who had sewn the quilt.

Now that she had the time frame, the names, and the town, it was time to find the family. From maps, she discovered that the town of South Apalachin was now the southeast part of the town of Owego, located in Tioga County in southeastern New York, right on the Pennsylvania border. *Apalachin* means "from where the messenger returned" in the language of the Lenape Indians of that area.

Melissa searched first for Jane Blair, Achsa Bancroft Moe, Lucy Wood, and Roy Wood and, using Ancestry.com, she was able to match the family name with South Apalachin. The dates also matched the quilt's fabric dates.

Searching the 1850 U.S. census, she found Jane Bancroft, her sister, Achsa Bancroft Moe, their sister, and their parents. She also found several other names familiar from the quilt, but sometimes she found more than one person by the same name. The historical society had sent her an 1865 plat map that showed who lived where, and Melissa says, "Once I established that this person lived two doors down from the quilt owners' home, I was pretty sure I had the right family."

Since all of the signatures were of women, Melissa also had to establish whether the names on the quilt were maiden names or married names. This challenge turned out to be more of a clue than a problem. "Once I found a young lady's name in the record and established who her parents were, I was able to establish birth records and marriage records," she says. And by comparing the names on the quilt with the marriage dates, Melissa was able to narrow the time frame of the quilt to the three-year period of 1855–1858.

Melissa had many unanswered questions, but time had run out, and her research assignment was due. She wrote up what she had found, but shared that there was still much to learn. Melissa received an A for her paper and encouragement from her professor to continue her research. However, she had exhausted all the work that she could do from Nebraska. It was time for a road trip, and Melissa knew the perfect traveling companion: her father, who happily agreed to accompany her.

Technology would continue to play a large role in the research of the quilt. "I didn't realize how mountainous the region was. It gave me a much better sense of the lives that these people would have lived," Melissa says. "We were traveling on a dirt road, which sometimes you do when you're following a GPS system, and looking for a cemetery. We couldn't find it. Suddenly my father laughed and pointed above us to a mountainside with headstones sticking out of the snow." They tramped uphill through the snow and found Bancroft family headstones as well as headstones for other names from the quilt. Melissa had checked the cemetery's listings on the Internet, but these names were not included. It was then that she realized she could not totally rely on information provided on the Internet.

Between records, cemetery trips, and visits to neighboring counties, she felt she had established where the Bancroft family had lived, but she could not find Jane Bancroft Blair herself. "I knew that she was, at that time, thirty-five years old and still single, but I couldn't find her anywhere."

*As Melissa explained who she was and what she was seeking, Ethel got a big smile on her face.*

The International Quilt Study Center and Museum.

As Melissa and her father prepared to return home, Melissa's father asked her if she had tried to trace the family forward to the present day. She hadn't. "I knew where Lucy had gone with her family, and I traced her forward through probate records. I reached a point three generations down where the person was young enough to still be alive," she says. The records included a telephone number for the descendant, Cheryl Klingensmith. Cheryl wasn't home when Melissa called, but her husband suggested Melissa speak with Cheryl's aunt, Ethel Wood. Ethel loved to talk about family history.

Melissa realized she was only a few blocks from Ethel Wood's small white house in Endicott, New York. A tiny lady with curly, white hair greeted her when she knocked.

As Melissa explained who she was and what she was seeking, Ethel got a big smile on her face and said, "Come on in and tell me all about it!" While they sat in her dining room drinking coffee and eating homemade cookies, Ethel talked about her family.

Ethel Wood turned out to have a direct connection to the quilt and its handwritten note. She was the eighty-eight-year-old widow of Leland Wood, who was the son of Roy Wood, the last name on the note.

Several items remained from Roy Wood's estate, including quilts, pictures, and a family Bible. Ethel was not sure what had happened to many of the things, but she thought the Bible was still around. She also suggested that Melissa contact her niece Cheryl again.

Melissa had mixed emotions as they headed back to Nebraska. She had gained a really good perspective on the history and culture of the area and pinned down all the names on the quilt, but she had not found Jane Blair Bancroft. "My ever-wise father told me to cheer up, because I'd found more than I thought I could. He said contacting the family always proved beneficial. And he didn't know how right he was."

Within two weeks of Melissa's return to Nebraska, Ethel Wood e-mailed her, saying, "Call me right away!" Ethel's daughter had visited her that day, and they had talked about Melissa's research. The two began searching through things and found the old family Bible, complete with births, deaths, and marriages going back many years.

Ethel began reading the information to Melissa over the phone faster than Melissa could write. The records were of the elusive Jane Blair Bancroft, her parents, and her siblings through the next generation. The Bible also contained labeled family photographs. Eventually, the family decided to donate the family Bible and the records to the IQSC so they could be with the quilt.

According to the information in the Bible, Jane's given name at birth was Mercy Jane Bancroft, born in 1825. The Bible listed Mercy Jane's marriage to Addison Blair, a widower with a son, in 1863. Mercy was thirty-eight years old when she got married, a spinster. Now knowing her husband's name, Melissa could move forward. She discovered that they had lived in Broward County, Pennsylvania, just across the New York border. Mercy Jane had joined Addison, his young son, and his parents in their home in South Hill, Pennsylvania.

The Broward County Historical Society referred Melissa to a local researcher, Norma Maryott, who proved to be very resourceful in finding data that wasn't on the Internet. "Norma remembered going to school with a lady that she thought was related to the Blairs. I called Ruth Smith and found out that she was the great-great-granddaughter of Addison Blair," says Melissa. Ruth became very interested in Melissa's research. She shared that the farmhouse and family farm still existed, but were no longer owned by the family.

Back in Pennsylvania, Ruth and Norma went for a Sunday drive to the old Blair farm. They explained their family history interests to the farm's new owners, Perry Cooley and his wife. Perry told them his father had been a hired hand on the property in the 1940s, working for Addison Blair's granddaughter. She was unmarried and had no children, so the farm was turned over to Perry's father, complete with furniture and a full attic.

Perry went to the attic and returned with an egg crate, which he gave to Ruth. The crate was a researcher's dream come true, filled with family photographs and thirty-two diaries written by Mercy Jane Bancroft Blair, which Ruth later donated to the IQSC. Many of the diaries had newspaper clippings, letters from family members, even hair clippings. Mercy Jane's diaries, which she wrote in religiously every day, included entries from January 1, 1859, through June 14, 1900, just a few days before she died. From these, Melissa learned that Mercy had been a traveling seamstress, moving from house to house as she worked. Mercy recorded details of her daily life, her religious observances, and her work as a seamstress, midwife, and nurse.

Mercy Jane also wrote of quilting, both for her clients and herself. A September 1863 entry reads, "Sister Moe helped me work on my quilt today and we finished it." She also wrote of finishing the binding on the quilt just before her November 1863 marriage.

Melissa thought that the quilt Mercy Jane completed just before her wedding was the very friendship quilt she had been researching. She suspected Mercy Jane made the quilt to help her remember old friends as she embarked on her married life. To test her theory, Melissa compared the handwriting in Mercy Jane's diaries to the transparencies and found them to be the same. Next, Melissa cross-referenced Mercy Jane's recorded sewing jobs with fabric used in the quilt. She found, for example, an entry reading, "Worked for Mrs. Brown today on her brown polka dotted dress & received 25 cents for same." The quilt contains a brown polka-dot block signed "Mrs. Elnina Brown."

The quilt shows little signs of use. Mercy Jane likely kept it tucked away after her marriage as a remembrance of her friends.

Melissa wrote her dissertation, "By God's Grave and the Needle: The Life and Labors of Mercy Jane Bancroft Blair," and was awarded her doctorate. Melissa says, "Given the resources, this is an exceptionally well-documented quilt now. There was this one little mystery that tugged on my heartstrings until it was solved. And it all started with one word on a piece of paper: *genealogy*." ❧

# SARAH FRANCES

There comes a time when we fade from memory and, for some, all that is left is a quilt. Sarah Frances Link lived from July 24, 1814, until July 27, 1879, in Person County, located in north central North Carolina. She outlived her husband and three of her children, including her daughter and namesake, Sarah Frances. Her only son, John, fought for the Confederacy and died shortly after the Civil War ended at the age of twenty-eight.

Sarah Frances could not read or write, which was not unusual for the times. She was a member of the Mill Creek Baptist Church, and her grave is in the church's cemetery with *Our Beloved Mother* engraved on her tombstone. It is believed that she created a hand pieced and hand quilted maroon and white Drunkard's Path quilt for her daughter Sarah Frances. The quilt's fabrics were probably dyed from natural materials on the farm, and the batting was probably homegrown and

*The Sarah Frances Quilt*
Drunkard's Path
Made by Sarah Frances Link (1814–1879), Person County, South Carolina
Circa 1870
72½ x 88½ inches
Cotton; hand dyed, hand pieced, and hand quilted
*Collection of Sarah Frances Tumblin Mantegna, photo by CMYK Photography*

hand-carded cotton; a few hull pieces can be found sticking out of the quilt.

Sarah Frances, the daughter, married Protheus Graves Montague on November 18, 1869. They lived on a farm in Granville County, one county over from Person. Sarah Frances died at the age of thirty-six, when her daughter Frances "Fannie" was only three years old. Protheus then married his deceased wife's younger sister, Elizabeth.

Perhaps the quilt survived when none others did because of the death. It was stored carefully away. Protheus had a luxuriant, full beard that would turn white with age and matched his hair. Elizabeth called him "Mr. Montague," both when speaking and referring to him, and he called her "Miss Elizabeth"—a very Southern practice. They lived together until their deaths a few weeks apart, when he was ninety-two and she was eighty-seven. They too were buried in the Mill Creek Baptist Church cemetery.

Fannie had dark, curly hair and blue eyes that sparkled. She was better educated than many girls in the rural South in those days. She finished school at the Oxford Female Seminary in Oxford, North Carolina, originally a Baptist institution.

Fannie married William "Will" Lewis Puryear in December 1897. Will was a tall, blue-eyed redhead who was four years older than Fannie. He was more deliberate and gentler in speech than his wife. Born in Granville, North Carolina, he did not have much more than a third-grade education, achieved in bits and pieces when he could be spared from the family farmwork. During their courtship, Will made Fannie a traditional split-oak melon-shaped basket with

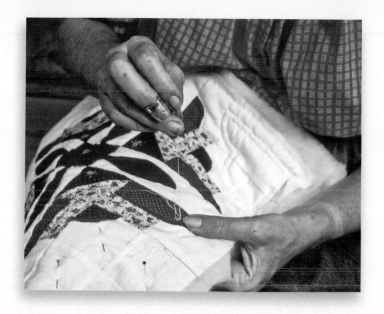

a sturdy handle. The basket is still intact and strong after more than one hundred years.

They started their life together with a team of mules, a wagon filled with whatever wedding and hope chest items they could get together, and fifteen dollars in cash. Their wedding trip was from her parents' home to their first farm in Buffalo Junction, Virginia. Sewing, crocheting, knitting, and quiltmaking were all things that Fannie did both from necessity and for beauty and creativity. Fannie and Will had eight children, but only four survived, one daughter and three sons—Edna, Erwin, Francis, and Eugene. The family eventually settled on a farm in Clarksville, Virginia. When Fannie's brother and his wife died, Fannie and Will also adopted their children: Martin, Mary, Billie, Charles, and John.

Fannie's daughter Edna never married. In addition to caring for her aging parents, helping her brothers and their families, and teaching piano, Edna liked to crochet tablecloths and bedspreads, and make quilts. After her parents died (Will in 1952 and Fannie in 1963), she stayed on in the big two-story farmhouse. (Each of Fannie and Will's children inherited one-fourth of the farm. Erwin and Eugene both moved back after they retired and lived on their inherited part of the farm.)

Edna was an independent woman. She bought a riding lawn mower and cut her own grass. Family members remember seeing her wearing a pair of pink slacks when she rode the mower. But even with her brothers nearby, Edna finally decided it was time to stop living alone. In 1979, she disposed of the household belongings and gave the family heirlooms and keepsakes to her brothers, her sisters-in-law, and their children. Edna's own quilts were also given to family members. She sold the house and land to her nephew and retired to the Culpepper Baptist Retirement Center. Unfortunately, before her nephew could move in, the farmhouse was burned to the ground, probably by vagrants. The tin roof lay crumpled on the ground, and the big oak tree that grew next to it was so scorched that it died the next year. Edna died of pneumonia in November 1989 at ninety years old.

Erwin married Jehu Louise Wall Tuten, known as Louise and eventually by her grandchildren as Boo. Erwin, known as Pop, was called to the ministry. He met Louise while he was enrolled in the seminary in Louisville, Kentucky. Pop was a tall man standing six foot four inches. He had bright red hair in his youth. In contrast, Louise was short, around five feet four inches, with dark hair and dark eyes. Pop had a sharp-edged teasing demeanor, while Louise was soft and loving. They lived in the tiny hamlet of Singer's Glen, Virginia, in the mountains outside of Harrisonburg.

Pop's arrangement with the church was to work four Sundays a month, so on the months with a fifth Sunday, he would have a day off. On those weekends, he would often travel to Clarksville and his portion of the family farm. On his portion of the farm, he

*Sarah assumed that her grandmother had made the quilt for her until her grandparents shared the story.*

built a modern brick home with a fish pond and log barn. Pop always had a large garden, some cows, and fruit trees. After he retired from the church in Singer's Glen, he and Louise lived for nearly twenty years in Clarksville, gardening, fishing, and participating in interim pastor duties around the area. Louise died in 1989, and Pop joined Edna at the retirement center just a few months before she died. He died in October 1996 at the age of ninety-three.

Erwin and Louise's daughter Alice Montague Puryear and her husband, John Tumblin, had a baby girl in 1958. The baby was named after John's favorite aunt, Sarah, and his mother, Frances. When Fannie Puryear learned of the birth and the name, she was pleased that her great-granddaughter had "been given a family name." Fannie told her daughter, Edna, and son, Erwin, that this newest Sarah Frances should be the one to inherit "the quilt." Fannie died five years later. Sarah has only a dim memory of her great-grandmother sitting on the back porch of the family farmhouse with Aunt Edna, snapping beans from the garden.

In 1976, the family gathered to celebrate Sarah's high school graduation. Her grandparents, Erwin and Louise Puryear, brought her a special gift. When Sarah opened the present, she discovered a quilt made in her high school colors— maroon and white. She assumed that her grandmother had made the quilt for her until her grandparents shared the story of the quilt. The family refers to the quilt as the *Sarah Frances Quilt*. Sarah could not recall ever having seen the quilt before that day, but Sarah's mother remembers it as a special quilt that was not often used but "kept for company" in a cedar chest.

At some point in time, both Fannie and Edna signed the quilt as a way of making it an important family heirloom and to create a link to the family's third Sarah Frances. Fannie would sign *F. G. Montague* on the front twice, and Edna would sign *Edna Puryear* on the back twice. It was assumed that the two signings happened at different times.

The quilt was in such great condition that Sarah questioned its true age. When she began learning to quilt in 1997, she asked her teacher, Holly Anderson, who was also a certified appraiser, to give her impressions. While Holly did not conduct an official appraisal, she did verify that the quilt had to have been made in the late 1880s.

Sarah Frances Tumblin Mantegna has continued the tradition of keeping the *Sarah Frances Quilt* for company. The quilt will continue to be stored in a safe place until it is passed on to Sarah's only daughter, Bonnie Louise. So far, there is not another Sarah Frances in the family, but who knows what the future will bring? ❧

# SUNDAY SCHOOL PICNIC

It was a brisk March day in New York in 1989. While it was not her first time attending a Christie's auction, it was the first time Shelly Zegart had held a bidding paddle in her hand. She was nervous and excited at the same time. Her mission was to purchase the *Sunday School Picnic* quilt, which was part of Sam and Nancy Starr's collection. The bidding went fast and furious. Every time the bid went up, so did her paddle, even though her husband kept trying to keep her arm down—30, 31, 35, 40, $41,800. Sold! The quilt now belonged to Shelly Zegart.

The 84¼-inch by 84-inch quilt was designed and made in 1932 by Jennie C. Trein in Nazareth, Pennsylvania. This kind of pictorial quilt was rare before the mid-twentieth century. For Shelly, the appeal was the storytelling aspect and that it was truly an iconic piece of art. Several objects in the quilt are

---

*Sunday School Picnic*
Designed and made by Jennie C. Trein (1879–1977), Nazareth, Pennsylvania
1932
84¼ x 84 inches
Cotton, silk, and rayon; hand pieced, hand appliquéd, embroidered, and hand quilted
Formerly in the collection of Shelly Zegart
*Collection of the Art Institute of Chicago, Robert Allerton and Christa C. Mayer Thurman*
*Textile Endowments (2001.450), photo by Geoffrey Carr*

three-dimensional: the log cabin and many of the aprons. It is embroidered with cotton, silk, and rayon, and covered with a wide variety of embroidery stitches. There is even a plastic Liberty Bell. Hand quilted with cotton with twelve stitches to the inch and backed with a plain cotton fabric, it is a unique expression of Jennie's life experiences.

Shortly after the Christie's auction, a curator who had been in attendance asked Shelly about "the letter." For some reason, the letter had not been transferred with the quilt at the time of the sale. And while the quilt had been published in magazines and featured in calendars, not much had been shared about the maker, so Shelly had no knowledge that a letter existed. Shelly was now on a mission to find and own the letter. She started to do some digging. The employees at Christie's did confirm that the letter had accompanied the quilt, but to Shelly's surprise, they did not want to give it to her. Finally, Shelly argued, "If I had bought a diamond you would have given me the appraisal with the diamond after I paid for it."

Christie's eventually agreed, and when the letter finally arrived, Shelly and her assistant read it while sitting on the floor in front of the quilt and trying to locate the different items and people mentioned. "The quilt took on a whole new life," Shelly says. "All those amazing facts would have been lost without the letter."

Shelly learned that Jennie made her first quilt when she was only ten years old and was still making quilts at the age of eighty-five. She died in 1977 at the age of ninety-eight. Over her lifetime, she completed more than one hundred quilts, and her children often wore clothing that she had made for them. A high-energy woman with many interests, Jennie played the piano, sang in her church choir for more than sixty years, and taught Bible classes for more than thirty years. She was also a member of the Women's Christian Temperance Union, an organization whose members were concerned about the destructive power of alcohol and the problems it was causing their families and society. They met in churches to pray, then marched to saloons to ask owners to close their establishments. The organization was established in 1874 and still exists today.

The letter, written on January 31, 1964, was not addressed to anyone. It said (shared here exactly as it was typed and written):

Mrs. Jennie C. Trein
33 E. Center Street
Nazareth, Pennsylvania

January 31, 1964

In the early summer of 1932, I, Jennie C. Trein maiden name Achenbach, was visiting with a dear friend, Mrs. Seyfried by name, at her country house which was in reality a log cabin - "a cottage by the site [*sic*] of the road."

The spacious enclosed porch was well furnished with comfortable old fashioned rocking chairs which were never allowed to cool off. Since we were busily engaged in designing quilt patches - the main design being a Dolly quilt.

And - 'tho my hands were busy I looked out into the orchard where was a hand made table, from which we ate the world famous cooking of the Pennsylvania Dutch such as "Snitzun Knepp, Rival soup, home cured ham with beans, parsnips, all sorts of pies, Dutch cake etc. etc. etc.

Then and there my thoughts ran into space. To design and make (for myself) A SUNDAY SCHOOL PICNIC QUILT. - First of all a foundation must be laid with the green (grass) combining with the sky of blue and that to be fit with Orion's belt, the big dipper and - the crescent. The red and blue birds and -tree, which must be buttonholed on. Since I was a tailoress in my teans [*sic*], I know how to work them. Please find geese above the log cabin and a boy shooting at them.

To the left of the cabin you will see two spooners pulling out when they decided - to elope on horse back.

There under a tree are cows enjoying the shade and a deer is leaving on the other side of a mound.

Find a little girl watering the plants with the sprinkling can. This was an easy task with the pump near by.

Notice the cat family on the stoop enjoying their supper.

With the flower bed in sight let us form a unique and beautiful picture of our sister country. The Holland Dutch. See the lake and wind wheels at the top. The boats coming from Holland and a party of bon voyage wishers are seeing their friends off to America.

In the woodland find an owl who is whooping, while the dog is near the comfort it.

We must now return to the Sunday school picnic which is held on the church lawn. The church roof, as also the sides, are made with the material suited as stucco slate roof and the painted fence is just white and green striped percale Cut to the slope of the cemetery. The church window sashes, door hinges, and the steps and the tops of the fence are all buttonholed. The tombstones all have initials, marked on, while only one is names for our ex president who is still living - HT. [Note: This must be Howard Taft.]

The picnic supper is about to be launched while the guests are arriving. Only a few dishes with a few pieces of watermelon as of now, grace the table and a little boy with his hands clasped on his back is asking "when do we eat?".

Find a mother (Mrs. Achenbach) to your right, bringing a loaf of home made bread, which was her speciality. She is dressed exactly as I used to see her since my childhood wearing a sunbonnet, a calico dress with a ruffle at the bottom, a gingham apron over, "never a white apron" and coat and see her high button shoes. Now we turn to the left of the table where we see my mother-in-law (Mrs. Trein) likewise wearing a sunbonnet, a gingham dress and - to be sure only a <u>white</u> apron would do for a picnic. Button shoes and her speciality; the coffee pot. A young man is chopping wood for the fire in the hearth which is in progress.

A young boy is bringing home the cows and ahead of him see a girl walking to a boy riding his pony - find the details worked on the cows tail and the main on the pony. Find two boys playing ball and ignoring a little boy who wished to join them. The girl wearing a mantilla, a mother and her little boy in bloomers as also the city lady with her fancy who is so disgusted with these country Rubes - that she went home.

To the lower right corner see our next door neighbors who never walked to church, side by side, but like geese going to water. Likewise to the picnic is Ed, Maria and Lizzy.

The kissing ring is in progress and my daughter (Martha Elizabeth), now a registered nurse, is overseeing the game. She too, is anxious for her coffee and together with her dog Buddy sees the sun is about to lower in the western sky.

See the big boob trying to get into the ring while they really don't want him. Also find the little girl wearing dainty pantalettes - trying to coach the little boy to enter the ring. But he flatly refuses by clasping his hands behind him. His little dog wonders "Why don't you want to go in?"

The cross road sign - To the Picnic is being observed by all who are coming (around the quilt border).

With no two dressed alike and many carrying umbrellas, fancy cakes decorated on high stands, baskets filled with celery carrots etc. - all make up for a most unforgettable Sunday School Picnic.

May I ask you to wear a critical eye and examine the dainty little belts, pockets and cuffs on the sleeves and not forgetting the trimmed hats of many designs. Find me with my twin girls which are not dressed alike. Also see where I am shaking hands with my neighbor. My twin girls were named Marie Ellen and Martha Elizabeth.

I can truly say my own designing of the *Picnic Quilt* is the only one in the whole wide world and therefore very special. A word about myself. From youth to the age of eighty five years has been a life full of various activities. Before I was ten years old I made a full size bed quilt by hand. When I reached my teens I was interested in music. I took vocal lessons and sang in church choirs for over sixty years. I still sing with our Nazareth Choral Society, December 1963. I play the piano and took to the cornet at the age of 44 years. Taught an adult Bible class in Sunday school plus a Bible class in my home for thirty years. The young girls then attending are now grandmothers but some of them teach in their respective Sunday schools. I am a member of the Womens Christian Temperance Union and have served as the recording secretary for thirty years. Really belong over fifty years. I married in 1902 and had four children for whom I made all their clothes until reached the teens. I never had any help, save for six months when I came home after a major operation. I made fare [*sic*] over a 100 quilts (for sale and gifts), over three hundred rugs since 1938. The little villages shown at Kutztown about sixty or more. So you may know mine was a very busy life and which I still am. In January 1964 I have already made a new quilt for myself. I was born February 18th, 1879 - and that leaves me at - 85, in a few weeks. The Dutch folk festival will take place from July 3rd through July 11th, 1964. Now that I was true to my promise in writing the description plus letting you know about the Kutztown festival I truly wish you to tell me how you liked my write-up as it leaves me on this 31st day of January 1964. I remain,

Loyally yours,
IN JESUS GLAD SERVICE
Jennie C. Trein

Shelly Zegart's introduction into the world of quilts began when she met Bruce Mann, who bought and sold quilts, in 1977. Bruce was from Louisville, Kentucky, where Shelly, originally from Pennsylvania, had settled. When she saw his quilts, "It was like magic for me. I wanted them all." In 1980, Shelly began seriously collecting quilts. She eventually would buy and sell quilts to gain financial independence. The issue was not about having enough money. Instead, it had to do with intellectual freedom, which translated into purchasing power. If she had the money, she could make decisions without input from her husband, Kenny. "I'm sorry you don't like it. That's okay, I still want it," explains Shelly.

In November 1980, Bruce was killed in an automobile accident at the age of 36. Before his death, Bruce had written a paper proposing an exhaustive study of Kentucky quilts, which would conclude with an exhibition. He had given the paper to Eleanor Bingham Miller, who brought the idea to Shelly. The

whole concept of the Kentucky Quilt Project, Inc., the first state quilt documentation project, was conceived at Shelly's kitchen table in early 1981. It would generate books and exhibitions that would inspire other states to do similar projects.

It was important for Shelly to secure the future for her quilts, which she always considered "on loan" to her. In 2001, *Sunday School Picnic* and the letter, along with twenty-seven other quilts from Shelly's collection, were acquired by the Art Institute of Chicago. In 2004, the quilts were part of an exhibition, *Exploring Quilts: Art, History and Craftsmanship*, at the Art Institute of Chicago. On the last night of the exhibition, as Shelly walked through the gallery, she felt both pride and sadness. ✍

# LADIES READING CIRCLE

The first Sunday of every month, the Mid-American Flea Market in Hutchinson, the largest indoor flea market in Kansas, is held. Fifteen years ago, in 1996, while Linda Laird was wandering through the flea market, a sweet signature quilt with embroidery made with prints from the 1930s caught her eye. It was ragged at the bottom, the binding was worn, and it was covered with grease stains. Linda suspected it was probably used in the back of someone's pickup truck. However, she thought she could get it clean enough to use for her purpose, and the price was right—less than $20.

Linda cut off the damaged last row of blocks, put a new, wider white binding over the worn-out white binding, and threw it in the washing machine to get it clean. She had bought the quilt to cover a cushion in a bedroom window seat that faced south. The removed portion of the quilt with its names and embroidery was saved and placed in a drawer. "I did

**Signature quilt**
Maker unknown, used for fundraising, Lewis, Kansas
Circa 1940
78 x 80 inches
Machine and hand pieced, embroidered, and hand quilted
*Collection of Linda Laird, photo by Linda Laird*

everything wrong with this quilt simply because I did not know any better at the time," she says.

The 78-inch by 80-inch quilt has *1940* embroidered in two places on the quilt. At the top in large embroidered letters is *ABW*. The white sashing is unusually large to allow room for names and embroidered images. The back is plain white fabric, not from feed sacks. The back also has some stains, including black grease stains in one corner. The piecing was mostly done by machine, but some was done by hand. The hand quilting was done straight across, then diagonally across the other way. It appears to have been stitched by several people and not evenly, as the stitches are of varying lengths. The cotton batting is crumpled because it's been washed so many times. Some of the embroidery stitches are missing. Many of the colored triangles do not meet in the middle. "It was a quick-and-dirty quilt except for the name blocks, some of which were so carefully done. What fascinates me is the embroidery. Each block is unique and some are just beautiful," says Linda.

Linda has always been a collector, but it wasn't until the early 1990s, when she returned to Kansas to help take care of her mother, that she began collecting quilts and quilt blocks. While living in Arizona, there simply were not many quilts available to collect. Her quilt collection has since grown to seventy quilts and more than seventy sets of quilt blocks. Linda even makes quilts to show off her other collections. So far she has completed a pot holder collection quilt and an antique belt buckle collection quilt. Eventually, she plans to make a doily collection quilt and a handkerchief collection quilt.

In a letter to her mother in 1961, when she was nineteen and living in Los Angeles, she wrote that she and a friend were going to make quilts and sell them. In her next letter, she wrote, "Making a quilt is much more difficult than we realized. I may have to buy a pattern." Linda can't remember if she ever finished that particular quilt, but she has made many over the years. In her quilt collection are quilts made by two of her great-grandmothers and two from her grandmother. Her own mother did not take up quiltmaking until she retired. She vowed to make a quilt for each of her children and grandchildren, which she accomplished. She died peacefully in her sleep at the age of ninety-three, with a finished quilt at her side for a neighbor's new baby.

In February 2004, Linda helped form MOKA (Missouri, Oklahoma, Kansas, and Arkansas) a group with membership from those four states that meets quarterly to study quilts. Linda joined the American Quilt Study Group shortly after MOKA was formed and then, inspired by the documentation of eighteenth-century signature quilts done by quilt historian and Kansas Quilt Project's cofounder Nancy Hornback, Linda decided to document her own signature quilt.

With more than 900 members, Linda's quilt guild seemed like the best place to start gathering information on her quilt. The Prairie Quilt Guild in Wichita, founded in 1982, holds two meetings, one in the afternoon and the other in the evening, on the second Tuesday of every month at the Wichita Downtown Senior Center. Linda shared the quilt and asked for help during the Show 'n' Share part of both meetings. It was suggested that *ABW* probably stood for

"American Baptist Women," ministries for girls and women in American Baptist Churches.

Linda carefully gathered the forty-five names on the quilt, then called the Baptist Churches in Hutchinson. No one recognized any of the names. Still determined to find a lead, Linda decided to go back to her guild for help. This time, she placed a small article in the guild's newsletter, which included all the names on the quilt. Three people contacted her. They had recognized the names.

The quilt was from Lewis, Kansas, about eighty miles west of Hutchinson. Lewis has always been a small town just off Route 50 in Edwards County (southwest Kansas). Edwards County's claim to fame is that it is the halfway point between San Francisco and New York City. The town was named after M. M. Lewis, a rancher and newspaper editor. *Lewis Press*, the town's newspaper, operated from 1904 until 1995, when it merged with the *Kingsley Mercury* to become the *Edwards County Sentinel*. The town's population in 2009 was only 444 people. Linda called town librarian, Mary Cross, who knew several names on the quilt, including Lucille Hiller and Esther Mead, both first cousins of her father. "Librarians are often much better than Google," says Linda.

The seed that would grow into the Meadowlark Library was planted in February 1911, when the Ladies Reading Circle was formed with fifteen charter members. Membership in the organization was by invitation only, and all members were from families that were community leaders. Also, several were working women. They voted to meet weekly, selected green and white as their colors, and set dues at $1 per year. After selecting to study American literature for their first year, they began by using the traveling library from Topeka. The next few years were formative ones, while the group conducted a study of libraries, held book showers, and organized a library committee. In 1917, the group voted to meet every other week and to join the Great Federation of Women's Clubs.

During the 1930s, having founded more than 474 free public libraries and 4,655 traveling libraries, women's clubs were credited by the American Library Association with establishing 75 percent of America's public libraries. The Meadowlark Library was formally organized in 1925 by the group, and Amy Bacon Wells, who was instrumental in many of the efforts in Lewis, served as the first librarian, retiring in 1959.

Mary knew immediately that the initials *ABW* were for Amy Bacon Wells. She explained that members of the Ladies Reading Circle made quilts to raise funds so that they could purchase books for the library. She also knew of two other similar signature quilts in town. All the women who had signed were deceased, except one, and she was in a nursing home. Linda immediately drove to the nursing home, fearing the woman would die before imparting any knowledge of the quilt. While Dorothy "Dot" Brumfield McLean was happy to see her, she had no knowledge of the quilt or of signing her name, and she said, "I certainly did not do any embroidery." Upon closer examination of the signature of her mother, Nell Brumfield, and the embroidery work, they both came to the conclusion that her mother had signed and embroidered Dot's name. When Linda mentioned that it was suggested that *ABW* had stood for American Baptist Women, Dot immediately replied, "My mother would never have associated with anyone who was Baptist. Those initials belong to Mrs. Wells, the town's librarian."

Linda's research would uncover other mother-daughter pairs on the quilt: Grace and Margaret Batman, Mabel and Gladys Sibley, Susi and Lucy Bridges, Mae Wells and Zena. Then there are mother-in-law and daughter-in-law pairs: Amy Bacon Wells and Zena, and Archie (named after her father) Rollins and Dorthea Rollins.

Two signatures and blocks are by members of the original library board: Cora Dugger and Augusta Meckfessel. Cora and William Warren (W. W.) Dugger moved to Lewis in 1909. They hired an architect from Dodge City to design a two-story house with a gambrel roof. W. W. managed the Farmers Coop Grain and Lumber Company. The Duggers liked children and every year had a big picnic for the town children at Elm Mills, a recreation spot near Medicine Lodge, eighty miles from Lewis.

Augusta Meckfessel was married to pioneer physician F. G. (Frank Gerhardt) Meckfessel. He began his practice in Albert, Kansas, where he met and married Augusta. The family moved to Lewis in 1920. Dr. Meckfessel traveled on foot, by saddle horse, by horse and buggy, on a motorcycle, and then by automobile to care for his patients.

Linda was quite curious about the other historic quilts that resided in the town, so she looked up the owners. She discovered that the quilts were very different both from hers and from each other. One quilt was made up of sunflowers with twenty petal points and embroidery that says, "Sunflower

Quilt, Meadowlark Library, 1943." People paid ten cents to sign their names in pencil—including Billy Cross, who was seven years old at the time—then the names were embroidered. Names of businesses were in the center of each sunflower and on the sashing. Names of individuals were on each petal point. The embroidery work on this quilt appears to be done by one individual who did not embroider well. The quilt ended up with Augusta and Dr. Meckfessel. When their daughter, LaVerne Slentz, was leaving town, she wanted the quilt to stay in Lewis, so she offered the quilt to LaVeda Bernstorf Cross. LaVeda did not feel right about just taking the quilt, so she paid for it. She hopes to donate it to the Edwards County Historical Museum. LaVeda was also a member of the Ladies Reading Circle.

The other quilt, which was dated 1936, was a Chimney Sweep block quilt with "Ever Faithful Sunday School Class" (of the Methodist church) embroidered on it. The quilt was quilted, but never finished. It has no binding. One name on the quilt is of a person who was born well after the date on the quilt. Why the name was added and the reason the quilt was not finished remain a mystery. The class was active within the community at the time, but it no longer exists.

Linda's research into the Ladies Reading Circle's newsletters never revealed any news on any of the quilts, and only once did she find a mention of any quilt. In researching for this story, one name (Lulu Derley) that could not be read because the embroidery was partially missing has been uncovered. Linda continues to research and shares, "Some people just get lucky. I did." As far as the Ladies Reading Circle, unfortunately, it disbanded in 1984 due to lack of interest. ❧

# A FORGOTTEN QUILT

In 1966, one month after graduating from college, Julie Silber followed two college friends, Pat Ferrero and Linda Reuther, to San Francisco, California. Julie had grown up in Detroit, Michigan, in an upper-middle-class family of first-generation Americans. While her parents were art collectors, quilts had not been a part of her world.

When Julie walked into Pat's home, she saw on the wall a large Victorian barn raising silk Log Cabin quilt in mauves, gray, and raspberry. Julie was stunned by its graphic beauty. "I will remember it forever. That moment changed my life forever," says Julie. Pat had purchased the quilt at a thrift store for $11. It was falling apart—pieces of it were actually on the floor—but this did not take away from its beauty. Pat explained the history as they set off to visit Linda.

At Linda's house, Julie found a 1930s Basket quilt folded neatly at the end of Linda's bed. Linda explained that it had been made by her grandmother and that the quilt was one of

---

**Baby quilt**
Made by Merry Silber, Michigan, possibly from a kit
1944
34 x 44 inches
Cotton; hand pieced and hand quilted
*Collection of Julie Silber, photo by the Quilt Complex*

her most prized possessions. So within a matter of a few hours, Julie had experienced the visual impact, the history, and the emotions produced by quilts. She was hooked!

When she began her life in San Francisco, she had two jobs at once. She was a performing musician, playing gigs downtown until 2 a.m. Waking at 6 a.m. during the weekdays, she taught nursery school from 7 a.m. to 2 p.m. This double-job life lasted nearly three months, until she fell ill with mononucleosis. She had to make a choice, and she chose the life of a teacher, but quilts were on her mind.

It was not easy finding quilts to purchase. If they were in thrift and antique stores, they would often be found balled up in a corner. Inquiries would often be met with, "Oh, yeah, I have a couple of quilts at home. Come back tomorrow." Julie did not have a lot of extra money, so she would only purchase a quilt if it cost less than $45.

Julie would eventually move into a place with Linda on 28th Street. One day the *Midwest Antique Trader* was mistakenly placed in their mailbox. It actually belonged to a resident one block over. Julie's curiosity got to her. She had not seen this kind of publication before. It had pages and pages of ads, so she began searching for quilts. She found a Double Wedding Ring quilt for $50 advertised and decided to buy it even though it stretched beyond her budget. When it arrived, she was delighted. The quilt had pink fabric instead of the usual white. With the thrill of the purchase under her belt, she decided to place an ad seeking quilts to buy and see what would happen. Before she knew it, her mailbox was filled with offers of quilts for sale.

The Lancaster Quilt & Textile Museum.

When a close friend of Julie's became pregnant, Julie decided to make her a simple baby quilt. There were not many books or patterns available to help her, so she went to the library and got Margaret Ickis's *Standard Book of Quiltmaking*. The quilt was composed of simple squares made with the typical calicos of the 1960s: red, blue, and yellow. With the making of this quilt, Julie realized, "I am the worst sewer ever." Looking back, however, she realizes now that "the process of quiltmaking is creatively very similar to the work that I do. When I do quilt exhibitions, organize books about quilts, it is the same format: You're taking disparate objects from out there and you're pulling them together and trying to put them into a coherent whole. So to some extent, I think I understand the process, and I think that I'm in tune with the process. But, I don't actually hold a needle and you wouldn't want me to."

*Since Linda and Julie loved everything about the experience, they suddenly decided that they wanted to have a shop.*

By this point, her house was filled with quilts. When Julie invited her mom to visit, Merry's reaction to quilts was exactly the same as Julie's had been. "It hit her hard," says Julie. Merry began by finding quilts in Michigan for Julie. Eventually, she would spend more than thirty-five years creating her own collection of quilts, working as an appraiser, helping to build private and public collections, and curating thirty-one exhibitions, including the first one in America devoted to Jewish quiltmaking. Merry assisted individuals in registering their quilts in the Michigan Quilt Project, founded quilt projects among senior citizen groups, collaborated on the design of numerous fund raising quilts, and delivered hundreds of lectures, including many on one of her favorite topics, the quilt blocks made to commemorate the Kindertransport, the rescue mission that sent thousands of Jewish children to safe refuge in Britain during World War II. Her antique quilt collection was donated to the Detroit Institute of Arts Museum, the Detroit Children's Museum, and the Michigan State University Museum in East Lansing, with the remainder given to Julie and family members. Merry donated a contemporary quilt, a recreation of the Wailing Wall in Israel, to the Fleischman Residence. The quilt has places for people to leave messages like the actual wall, and Julie has done so on several occasions. People traveling to Israel then take the messages and place them in the actual wall.

In 1970, Merry invited Linda and Julie to exhibit their quilts at a gallery in Birmingham, Michigan, where she worked as the print and lithograph expert. Unexpectedly, people came to the exhibition with hopes that Linda and Julie would purchase their antique quilts. "We bought some of our most treasured quilts during that show," says Julie. One of the quilts purchased was a fabulous trapunto Mariner's Compass quilt that was signed and dated "Mary R. Strickler 1834."

Since Linda and Julie loved everything about the experience, they suddenly decided that they wanted to have a shop. Neither had any business experience, but that did not stop them. In early 1972, they opened a quilt shop just north of

San Francisco in San Rafael. At Merry's suggestion, they named the shop Mary Strickler's Quilt and hung her quilt behind the counter for everyone to see.

While the shop sold antiques, its emphasis was on antique quilts, with 95 percent of its inventory being quilts. "We had about three hundred quilts at any time, and we were especially friendly and encouraging about people coming and feeling that they did not need to buy anything. In that way, the 'shop' also acted as a museum or gallery and as a meeting place for quilt lovers," Julie says. They closed the shop almost exactly ten years later, following the success of their first major museum show, *American Quilts: A Handmade Legacy*. They decided that instead of running a retail business, they wanted to devote their energies to curating museum exhibitions, lecturing, writing, and teaching about antique quilts and women's history.

After the shop closed, Doug Tompkins (cofounder and owner of the Esprit clothing brand, and the force behind the Esprit Quilt Collection) decided to offer Julie a job. He had been a customer from almost the opening of her shop, and Julie had helped him, informally, to organize the records on his collection. Now he asked Julie to formally take the job as curator. She agreed, but opted for working part time so she could also dedicate herself to the other quilt activities she wanted to do. She has worked with Esprit from 1982 to the present.

Doug began collecting quilts in the 1970s. The quilts' designs, shapes, and colors were reflected in all aspects of Esprit's brand, from hang tags to catalogs to the clothes themselves. His collection explores the changing art-historical understanding of quilts, from folk art to feminist expression to

American modernism. At the heart of the Lancaster Quilt & Textile Museum's permanent exhibition are eighty-two quilts from the Esprit Quilt Collection. Many scholars consider it to be the finest collection of authentic late nineteenth- to twentieth-century Amish quilts indigenous to the Lancaster region of Pennsylvania.

In 1995, Julie started her own company called The Quilt Complex, named for all the different services she offers revolving around antique quilts. In the beginning, Julie was able to bring Joe Cunningham from Vermont to help, and he continues to work with her. In 1996, Jean Demeter joined her as a partner. They buy and sell antique quilts, do appraisals, lecture, write, and curate collections and museum exhibitions.

One day in April 2010, when Merry was cleaning out her home in preparation for a move to the Fleischman Residence, she discovered in a box safely tucked away a baby quilt that she had made for Julie. She remembered that she had made it from a kit, but she could not recall the actual creation process. The simple quilt was once again reunited with Julie, and this discovery changed everything and nothing for both of them. ❧

# OLD MAID, NEW WOMAN

As a contributor to the *World of Quilts* exhibit, Shelly Zegart was invited and jumped at the chance to stay at Meadow Brook Hall, the former residence of Matilda Dodge Wilson. Matilda was the widow of automotive pioneer John Dodge, and her 110-room Tudor Revival home is representative of residences of the very wealthy in early twentieth-century America. The one-hundred-quilt exhibition, hosted by Oakland University in Rochester Hills, Michigan, ran September 8–25, 1983.

One evening during her stay, Shelly took the opportunity to wander around the home and get a closer look at the quilts on display. When she turned a corner, tucked away was a presentation quilt with the image of an old woman in the middle. It was so unlike the other quilts in the exhibition, which were older and more traditional. As she examined the

**Presentation quilt**
Made by members of the Young Ladies Sewing (or Aid) Society, Canandaigua,
  New York, for Susan Elizabeth Daggett
1871
68 x 76 inches
Cotton; hand pieced, appliquéd, and signed in ink
Formerly in the collection of Shelly Zegart
*Collection of the Los Angeles County Museum of Art (M.91.271), photo by Geoffrey Carr*

quilt further, her desire to know more intensified. The next day she asked Sandra Mitchell (one of the organizers) who owned the quilt. It turned out that it belonged to Joan Fenton and Albie Tabackman of Quilts Unlimited in West Virginia. Shelly told Sandra that if Joan and Albie ever wanted to sell the quilt, she was interested. In the summer of 1984, Shelly was offered the quilt, and it became hers.

When the quilt arrived, Shelly and her assistant, Dorothy West, immediately began examining it. They gathered the forty-three names on the quilt and read the penned inscriptions. "That you may be beloved be amiable, Susan the Matchless" and "Like a ring without a finger/Like a bell without a ringer/Like a ship which ne'er is rigged/Or a mine that's never digg'd/Like a wound without a tent/Or civent box which has no scent/Just such as these may she be said/That loves, ne'er loves but dies a maid./ A.B.R. [Anna B. Richards]" and "Dont laugh till you're entirely kilt/When you behold this gorgeous quilt/Kate B Antis 1871."

Shelly still has the piece of paper where she wrote, "Who was Susan Elizabeth Daggett?" Was she the woman on the quilt or just the original owner?

All the information needed to begin a search was on the quilt: names, location, Susie's full name, date of birth, and more. So the research began with a trip from Shelly's home in Louisville, Kentucky, to Canandaigua, New York, in late February 1985. The state of New York requires that every town have a town historian who is responsible for preserving the past. Ontario County Historical Society in Canandaigua, the New Haven Colony Historical Society, the Connecticut Historical Society, and the Yale Divinity School Library would provide Shelly with a wealth of information, as would the church records of the First Congregational Church in Canandaigua and the Second Congregational Church in New London, Connecticut.

Susan "Susie" Elizabeth Daggett was born on December 9, 1841, to Dr. Oliver and Elizabeth Watson Daggett. She was the oldest child of three. Her brother, Ellsworth, was born in 1845, and her sister, Mary, was born in 1851. Her father was the minister of the First Congregational Church of Canandaigua.

Susie's parents nurtured her in an intellectually stimulating environment. Among the notables of the day invited to speak at the church and stay with the Daggetts were Henry Ward Beecher, a prominent Congregational clergyman, social reformer, abolitionist, and speaker, and Edward Everett, a politician and educator from Massachusetts.

Susie, with many of her friends who would help form the Young Ladies Sewing Society, attended the Ontario

Female Seminary in town. Religion and the Bible were major parts of the curriculum. Susie was fourteen when Susan B. Anthony came to speak. Caroline Richards wrote in her diary: "She [Susan B. Anthony] made a special request that all the seminary girls should come to hear her as well as all the women and girls in town. She had a large audience and she talked very plainly about our rights and how we ought to stand up for them, and said the world would never go right until the women had just as much right to vote and rule as men. She asked all to come up and sign our names who would promise to do all in our power to bring about that glad day when equal rights should be the law of the land. A whole lot of us went up and signed the paper." This visit likely played a role in Susie's decision four years later to never marry.

> *Susie was eighteen years old when she declared to her friends that she would never marry.*

In December 1859, the young women of the First Congregational Church of Canandaigua, New York, formed the Young Ladies Sewing Society (also known as the Young Ladies Aid Society). The purpose of the group was "To cultivate, enrich, and ennoble our intellectual and moral natures, and to form habits of systematic benevolence in harmony with the divine precept 'To do good and to communicate—forget not' is the object contemplated by this organization." The projects included organizing fairs, holding a festival to benefit the library, furnishing funds for the Home of Friendless in New

York, sending many valuable boxes to needy ministers and families, and, during the Civil War, making items of clothing for Union soldiers. The group met every two weeks, the members taking turns as hostesses for the meeting. The group also agreed to present each member with an album bed quilt with all their names on it when each woman married.

Susie was eighteen years old when she declared to her friends that she would never marry. In Caroline Cowles Richards's diary entry of December 13, 1859, she wrote, "Susie Daggett says she is never going to be married, but we must make her a quilt just the same." Caroline Cowles Richards's diary, which she started at the age of ten and kept for twenty years, was published the first time in 1913 by Henry Holt & Co. as *Village Life in America 1852–1872*. It was reprinted in 1972 by Corner House Publishers in Williamstown, Massachusetts, and it is this edition that Shelly purchased in the Ontario County Historical Society's gift shop. The diary would prove invaluable to Shelly's understanding of Susie's life and the time in which she lived.

Shelly would uncover a startling fact: A substantial number of mid-nineteenth century American women chose to remain single. Like Susie, they boldly announced their intentions at the time when they would be expected to begin the rituals of dating and courtship. The reasons for remaining single were varied, but Susie certainly stayed true to her word. In 1871, just two years after Wyoming became the first state to give women the right to vote, Susie turned thirty. She was living with her parents in New London, Connecticut, when she received her promised album bed quilt from the ladies of the society.

Susie taught at Vassar College from 1871 to 1873 and returned in 1877. A photograph of Susie, taken in Poughkeepsie, New York, in 1878, when she was thirty-seven, shows her at a time when she held the position of Assistant Lady Principal of Vassar College. She left the position later that year. After looking at the photograph, it was obvious to Shelly that the central figure on the quilt did not represent Susie at all. In a booklet published by the First Congregational Church upon its one hundredth anniversary in June 1899, an essay on the church's young people sheds even more light on Susie's quilt:

> Any member reaching the age of thirty years, being still unmarried, was to receive a quilt. There is, however, a record of only one member, Miss Daggett, being brave enough to acknowledge the attainment of such great age. . . . Each member of the society made a block, containing her autograph, but in all probability the central block was the chief cause of this custom being forever abolished. This block, donated by the pastor, Mr. Allen, consisted of a pen-picture of a spinster with her knitting work, her hair done up in a ridiculous little knot. This, by the way, was not intended to be an exact likeness of any member of the society.

"One can only imagine the emotions this quilt must have aroused for it to be so thoroughly discussed twenty-eight years later," says Shelly. "As we study this quilt today, some of the penned inscriptions seem overly mean. But, since Susie's opinions on singlehood were so well known among her peers, and shared by at least some of their number, it is

Meadow Brook Hall.

unlikely that these inscriptions were meant to mock her. In fact, they may have been sly rebukes of old-maid stereotypes, 'in jokes' to a sister who would not only appreciate the double, hidden meanings behind the inscriptions, but delight in their creativity. That the quilt survives in such pristine condition is testimony that it was held very dear by its recipient." Shelly later discovered that twelve of the forty-three women on the quilt did not marry.

After Susie's father's death in 1880, Susie, along with her mother and sister, moved to New Haven, Connecticut, where her father had been born. Susie's paternal grandfather, David Daggett, had graduated from Yale in 1783, gone on to serve in the United States Senate, and, in 1826, returned to Yale to serve as Kent Professor of Law. Their return to New Haven may have been forced by finances. Susie's position at Vassar, though a respected one, probably was not lucrative.

At some point during her adult life in New Haven, Susie gave her quilt to Clara Wilson Coleman, a friend in Canandaigua, who was among the Society members who created it. The quilt passed to Clara's daughter, Susan Daggett Coleman, Susie's namesake. It found its way through that family to the Canandaigua First Congregational Church's 150th anniversary in 1949.

Susie was reported to be in excellent health her entire life. She fell ill only three weeks prior to her death in 1931 at the age of eighty-nine. Her obituary appeared in the Saturday, January 10, 1931, edition of the *New York Times*. It mentioned her lifetime of service to the church, mission work, and education. She was buried in Grove Street Cemetery near her home.

At the time of her death, Susie's estate was valued at nearly $100,000, no small sum in 1931. Susie stayed true to her beliefs. She left money to the Calhoun Colored School of Calhoun, Lowndes County, Alabama; to Piedmont College in Demorest, Georgia; to the Ecclesiastical Corporation of the First Congregational Church of Canandaigua for relief of the poor of the church; and to the New Haven YWCA in memory of her sister, Mary, with the stated preference that the income be used for giving the "privilege of classes to poor girls." At Yale, at her bequest and in memory of her father (B.A. 1828), the *Oliver Ellsworth Daggett Scholarship Prize* is awarded each year to a student who, at the end of the second year of study in the school, is in need of financial assistance and who is judged by the faculty to be most worthy in ability, diligence, Christian character, and promise of usefulness as a preacher. The scholarship prize is still awarded today.

It was important to Shelly that she share what she had discovered as part of her commitment to quilt scholarship. In 1986, an article on the quilt was published in *The Quilt Digest*. She continued to research the quilt well into 1989 and at one time had hoped to write a book. She exhibited the quilt whenever she was given the opportunity.

While Sandi Fox was the collection curator for quilts at the Los Angeles County Museum of Art, she convinced Shelly to donate the quilt to the museum. Sandy had high hopes that the museum would become the first quilt study center. Unfortunately, it did not happen. The quilt remains a part of the museum's collection, but is not on display. Shelly thinks that Susie would still be pleased. ❧

# HISTORY DIVIDED

Before Pat Ferrero began working on what would become her award-winning film *Hearts and Hands*, she and Julie Silber, who helped produce it, decided to consult some experts. This 1988 installment of the acclaimed PBS series *The American Experience* profiles women involved in some of the most crucial events of nineteenth-century U.S. history. Pat also chose to feature "more anonymous women who helped create this nation, and whose lives can be, to an extent, read in the art of their quiltmaking." After hiring Jonathan Holstein as a consultant for the day, Pat and Julie traveled from their homes in California to Jonathan's home in Cazenovia, New York, where he invited Marjorie Ayars Laidman to share her family's silk quilt with them.

The pieced silk quilt was attributed to Deborah Coates, Marjorie's great-great-great grandmother, and was probably made c. 1830–1860, although family history dates the quilt to before Deborah's marriage in 1819. The original quilt

---

**Birds in the Air**
Made by Deborah Coates, Lancaster County, Pennsylvania
Circa 1830–1860
89 x 96½ inches (original quilt before it was divided)
Silk with stamp work; hand pieced and hand appliquéd
*Collection of the Heritage Center of Lancaster County, photo by Pat Ferrero*

Detail of inked patch in the center block of quilt, 3 x 1½ inches.
*Photo by Pat Ferrero*

was 89 inches by 96½ inches, with more than one hundred blocks placed on point. The pattern is one of a variety of Sawtooth designs popular in the 1840–1864 era according to Barbara Brackman, author of *Quilts from the Civil War* (C&T Publishing, Inc., 2009). This time period was also the most active time for the Underground Railroad. Ruth Finley in her 1929 book *Old Patchwork Quilts and the Women Who Made Them* called the pattern Birds in the Air, Flying Birds, and Flock of Geese, and similar patterns are known as Sailboat or Corn and Beans. It seems unlikely that Deborah knew the pattern as Birds in the Air, but the family did not pass on the name.

According to the family, two of Deborah's granddaughters could not agree on who should inherit the precious family quilt, and so, with the Quaker sense of equality, it was decided to cut the quilt in half and rebind it. While everyone was admiring the two halves, "eagle-eyed Pat," according to Julie, noticed a tiny foot on one quilt half and the edge of an arm on the other that no one had seen before. "There is something here!" she exclaimed. Upon closer examination, it was agreed that something was indeed stamped with black ink on one of the quilt's many triangles.

Under the careful direction of a conservator, the bindings were opened and a stamped image of a man begging, on one knee, wearing shackles with the phrase "Deliver me from the oppression of man" underneath was revealed. The image is similar to a well-known British medallion designed by Josiah Wedgwood in 1787 for the Society for the Abolition of the Slave Trade. The image of the bound slave was incorporated into a wide range of popular commercial items, ranging from dishes to penwipes (used to clean drips off dip pens) to clay pipes to needle cases. The only significant difference is that Wedgwood's image is accompanied by text that reads, "Am I not a man and a brother?" While Wedgwood's phrase asks the nature of social conformity, the phrase on the quilt is a plea for safeguarding and certainly speaks to Deborah's life.

> *With the Quaker sense of equality, it was decided to cut the quilt in half and rebind it.*

Deborah was born Deborah T. Simmons on March 7, 1801, in Pennsgrove, Chester County, just west of Philadelphia and north of the Mason-Dixon Line, which forms the border between Pennsylvania and northern Maryland. Her family, members of the Religious Society of Friends (Quakers), had colonized Pennsylvania. At age eighteen, she married Lindley Coates, also a Quaker, in West Grove, Pennsylvania, on December 16, 1819. He was five years older and a farmer. Lindley was remembered by friend and poet John Greenleaf Whittier as "a tall gaunt man, erect, eagle-faced, upon whose somewhat martial figure the Quaker coat seemed a little out of place. [He was] known in all of Eastern Pennsylvania as a stern enemy of slavery."

The Coates family was well known in the early part of the nineteenth century. Lindley Coates was a prominent and active abolitionist. He was among the organizers of the Clarkson Anti-Slavery Society (1833) and preceded William Lloyd Garrison as president of the American Anti-Slavery Association from 1940 to 1943. As a member of the Pennsylvania Constitutional Convention in 1837, he sought to prevent the word *white* from being placed into law for the State of Pennsylvania in his unsuccessful attempt to grant black men voting rights.

In her early twenties, while living in Lancaster County, Deborah gave birth to three sons. It was during this time that there was enough dissension among the Quakers that slavery's "stern enemies" broke from the orthodox branch. These more radical Quakers were known as Hicksite Quakers after itinerant Quaker preacher Elias Hicks of Long Island, New York. Elias Hicks was one of the earliest abolitionists among the Friends.

An eloquent speaker, he spoke often about slavery and worked hard to persuade others to oppose it. Historian Beverly Wilson Palmer, who edited the letters of Quaker abolitionist Lucretia Coffin Mott, has identified Deborah Coates as a Hicksite Quaker minister. Many Hicksites advocated women's equality, and Deborah seemed to be an equal partner with her husband in both his religious life and the antislavery cause.

In researching the family history related to the quilt, a descendant discovered that Lindley and Deborah's home in Sadsbury, Pennsylvania, was Station No. 5 on one of the many routes of the Underground Railroad. Robert Clemens Smedley's 1883 book *History of the Underground Railroad in Chester and Neighboring Counties of Pennsylvania* confirms that the Coates house was used as a stop on the Underground Railroad. The Coates family was one of the first not only to see the evil in slavery but to realize that the law should be resisted.

Deborah's son Simmons married Emeline Jackson, and their Chester County farm became another stop on the Underground Railroad. In 1862, Simmons was killed by an overturned oxcart when he was forty-one years old. Deborah outlived her husband by more than twenty-five years and spent most of her widowhood living with her daughter-in-law, Emeline. Emeline never remarried and ran the family farm until her death in 1894. The 1880 census reveals the two widows living with three of Emeline's daughters and two grandsons, plus a black servant and her baby boy. At age seventy-eight, Deborah was the matriarch in a house of women and children.

Deborah's son Kersey moved to Kansas City, Missouri, in 1854. Known as an antislavery activist, he was active in the

Free State Movement during the Bleeding Kansas skirmishes with neighboring Kansas between 1854 and 1858. At the heart of the conflict was the question of whether Kansas would enter the Union as a free or slave state. Kansas would eventually enter the Union as a free state. Kersey also served as a colonel in the Civil War. He died in 1887. Deborah's son Comley was a mute. There is no record of what happened with him.

Deborah died on August 31, 1888. She and Lindley are buried next to one another in the West Grove Friends burial grounds in Chester County.

The quilt truly reflects Deborah's beliefs. For example, it is made of silk. Some Quakers believed that cotton and slavery were so interwoven that they refused to wear calico (cotton). Deborah might have used a piece of fabric stamped with a woodblock meant for paper printing to create the figure with its antislavery message.

The quilt was originally given to Simmons Coates and was then passed to his wife, Emeline, after his death. She then gave it to their daughter, Elizabeth Jackson Coates, who was born in 1846. Elizabeth married Marriott Brosius in 1869. In October 1861, Marriott had joined the Civil War and enlisted as a private in Company K, Ninety-seventh Regiment, Pennsylvania Volunteers, for three years before reenlisting in May 1864. He was wounded a few months later and was honorably discharged in December 1864. On February 28, 1865, he was commissioned a second lieutenant for bravery on the field of battle. He studied law and became an attorney. In 1890, he was elected as a Republican to the Fifty-first and to six succeeding Congresses. He died in 1901 at the age of fifty-eight, while still in office. Elizabeth died in 1907. They are buried together in Greenwood Cemetery in Lancaster.

The quilt was finally divided between Elizabeth's and Marriott's two daughters, Graceanna Brosius Biddle, the donor's maternal grandmother, and her sister Gertrude Coho Reinhartson, when they could not decide who should inherit the quilt. The two halves were then reunited when they were given to Marjorie Ayars Laidman. In 1986, with the help of Jonathan Holstein, the quilt was donated to the Heritage Center of Lancaster County. It remains in two pieces as an important reminder of a significant time in American history and a remarkable woman who should not be forgotten. ❧

# THE DOCTOR
# AND THE QUILTMAKER

After his birth in 1868 in Philadelphia, William Rush Dunton Jr.'s family influenced his career choice of psychiatry, and finding a book on quilts changed his life. His father, Jacob, was a pharmacist. His uncle William Rush Dunton was a physician, and another uncle, Benjamin Rush, is still often called the father of American psychiatry. After graduating from medical school at the University of Pennsylvania in 1893, William practiced at Johns Hopkins. He left Johns Hopkins to become an assistant physician at the Sheppard Asylum, the forerunner of today's Sheppard and Enoch Pratt Hospital.

William Jr. married Edna Hogan on July 1, 1897. They had three children. Early in his work with the mentally ill, he became fascinated by the healing potential of occupational therapy. He helped to form a society of occupational therapists,

---

**Iris**
Designed and made by Marie Webster (1859–1956), Marion, Indiana
Circa 1909
82 x 83 inches
Cotton and linen; hand pieced, hand appliquéd, and hand quilted
*Collection of Rosalind Webster Perry, photo by William B. Dewey*

which in 1917 became the National Society for the Promotion of Occupational Therapy. This group is now called the American Occupational Therapy Association. He credited Marie Webster for awakening his interest in quilts.

Marie Webster was born in 1859 in Wabash, a small town in rural northern Indiana. She was the oldest of six children. Marie's mother was an excellent needlewoman who taught her three daughters the sewing skills needed for domestic life. Marie attended local public schools and graduated at the top of her high school class. Though she was eager to attend college, health concerns prevented her.

*Dunton quickly realized that the process of making a quilt would be of great benefit to his "nervous ladies."*

In 1884, she married George Webster, a successful businessman, and the couple settled in Chicago. A few years later, the Websters moved to George's hometown of Marion, Indiana, at the time a manufacturing center in the state. George became a banker, and Marie's main hobbies became sewing and needlework.

Marie had been embroidering household linens since she was a child, but she did not make her first quilt until 1909, when she was fifty years old. She did not care for the geometric pieced quilts popular at the time, so she began to create her own floral appliqué patterns. In its January 1, 1911, issue, *Ladies' Home Journal* featured four of Marie's quilt designs in full color. With a circulation of more than 1.5 million readers, the feature made her a household name. Readers wrote her for patterns. Within one month of the *Ladies' Home Journal* publication, Marie was selling her quilt patterns for fifty cents each. In 1911 and 1912, her first fourteen quilts appeared in the magazine.

The demand for her patterns was so great that Marie decided to run a mail-order business from her home. The successful business became known as the Practical Patchwork Company and sold patterns, quilt kits, and even finished quilts. Her success caused the New York publisher Doubleday, Page & Company to invite her to write a book on the history of quiltmaking. Tracing the history back to ancient Egypt and up to America, the book was published in 1915 as *Quilts: Their Story and How to Make Them.* The highly successful book has gone through several editions and remains popular today. Included in the seventy-fifth anniversary expanded edition of Marie's other book, *A Joy Forever: Marie Webster's Quilt Patterns* (Practical Patchwork, 1990), is a new biography written by Rosalind Webster Perry, Marie's granddaughter.

It was Marie Webster who sparked Dr. Dunton's interest in documenting quilts and their history. Seeing the possibilities of quiltmaking as a therapy for his patients, Dr. Dunton began collecting anything that he could find about quilts— photographs, articles, patterns, and fabric samples. He also quickly realized that the process of making a quilt, as well as the social interaction that making quilts provided, would be of great benefit to his "nervous ladies." As a psychiatrist, he thought his female patients could profit from the quiet, calming influence of quiltmaking as well as the sense of accomplishment it brought. He began to document quilts owned by friends, relatives, and patients and those he saw at quilt fairs and contests.

According to Dr. Dunton in his 1946 self-published book, *Old Quilts*, his interest in quilts came "in 1915 after reading Mrs. Marie D. Webster's *Quilts: Their Story and How to Make Them*, altho it seems that I must have had an interest before that time or I should not have wanted to read the book." In the introduction to his book, he shares that he cannot recall any quilts in his home as a boy and speculates that "their making was too unfashionable in large cities to interest many during the 1870s." However, much later in life, when he came across a long-forgotten box in his closet, he wrote that he had found "a tea box of diamonds of colored silks in which I recognize some of my childhood neckties . . . and I believe I assisted in cutting these."

Dr. Dunton began corresponding with Marie shortly after her book was published. He ordered her patterns to use with his patients. Dr. Dunton held his first quilt exhibit for his patients at the hospital September 5–9, 1916, and he invited Marie to participate. The exhibit contained fifty quilts borrowed from the families of patients and friends, as well as six loaned by Marie. These were her Iris, French Basket, Wreath of Roses, Bedtime, Sunbonnet Lassies, and Butterflies and Pansies. (The pattern for her Iris quilt was one of the first that she published, and some of the pastel fabrics in the completed quilt were linen.) Marie also sent two pieces of Egyptian appliqué, possibly a gift from a friend, which were included in the exhibit. They are also mentioned and illustrated in her book. The September 5 headline in the *Baltimore American* newspaper was "Art Quilts on Display." Dr. Dunton went on to curate three quilt exhibits for the Baltimore Museum of Art, with the 1944 exhibit featuring Baltimore Album Quilts.

Dr. Dunton wrote to Marie again in the 1930s about the publication of her book when he was attempting to find a publisher for his own book, and he even paid her a short visit sometime between 1935 and 1937. He refers to his visit in a letter to Marie dated March 22, 1937: "It has been rather good fun to collect these names and designs, and some day I hope that you will drop in on me, as I did on you, so that we may have a pleasant gossip. I hope, however, that you will make your visit longer than I was able to make mine."

According to the Baltimore Museum of Art, where Dr. Dunton donated his collection:

The Dunton collection contains twenty-five linear feet of materials, plus six microfilm reels and twenty-nine volumes of photocopies, which were collected by Dunton during the years 1912–1957. A few linear feet of the collection are occupied by examples of the boxes and cartons in which the collection was originally contained.

Dunton's archives all relate to his personal interest in and study of quilts and other textiles in Maryland and around the United States. His collected research is found in many formats and includes photographs, fabric samples, correspondence, collected quilt patterns, and news clippings relating to quilting. He published only one book on this subject, *Old Quilts*, but wrote profusely. Therefore, his papers at the Baltimore Museum of Art contain unpublished manuscripts as well as short articles and research files on many textile related topics. A crowning achievement in his research are his scrapbooks which chronicle his studies over 45 years and offer to researchers documentation of hundreds of quilts that he had opportunity to view, photograph, and study.

Dr. Dunton amassed many volumes and documents relating to his research and organized them painstakingly. His research archives are now housed in the Textiles Department at the Baltimore Museum of Art. These papers have been at the Baltimore Museum of Art for an undetermined amount of time, but at least since his death in 1966, since the records themselves indicate that he prepared them specifically for donation to this institution.

Dr. Dunton's methods of recording and storing his research materials are of note. He often reused old file folders from his medical practice, leaving original file headings still present. He turned over work related flyers and papers and put his quilt notes on back. He used Kraft Caramel boxes to store his negatives, a B Complex vitamins box to hold some glass lantern slides, wooden hinged boxes for manuscripts, and old record album boxes to store his elaborate fabric samples catalog.

Marie's husband, George, died in 1938. When Marie moved out of her Marion home in 1942, she disbanded the Practical Patchwork Company and did not make any more quilts. That same year, she moved with her son and his family to New Jersey. She died in 1956, at the age of ninety-seven.

Dr. Dunton spent his professional life in Baltimore and died in December 1966 at the age of ninety-eight.

In 1979, Dr. Dunton was inducted into the Quilters Hall of Fame, and Marie Webster was inducted in 1991. At Marie's induction, Hazel Carter, founder of the Quilters Hall of Fame, met Rosalind Webster Perry, Marie's granddaughter. Just a few months earlier, Rosalind had rescued her grandmother's home from demolition, and within thirty minutes of the two meeting, Rosalind proposed that the Marie Webster house become the permanent location for the Quilters Hall of Fame. On June 17, 1992, the Marie Webster House was listed in the National Register of Historic Places, and, in 1993, the property was designated a National Historic Landmark. In 2004, the fully restored Marie Webster House opened as the headquarters for the Quilters Hall of Fame. ✍

# REPRODUCING THE PAST, TOUCHING THE FUTURE

Janice Paine Dawes's earliest memory of sewing was a potholder she made for her mother when she was seven or eight years old. Her mother had given Janice scraps to wrap around her dolls. She sneaked a needle, thread, and scissors to use, and to the basement she went with her treasures to create her masterpiece. She knew that potholders had something in the middle of the fabrics, so she collected dryer lint to stuff her creation. Thinking back, Janice says, "I'm sure she would have burned her hands if she had tried to use it!"

In 1969, she made her first "real quilt" for her first child, Michael Peters, from a pattern in a magazine. While she did use cotton batting, it was not needle punched so it fell apart when it was washed. The next time she was brave enough to try again was in 1973, when her daughter, Ginger Peters, was born.

---

**Variable Star and Nine Patch**
Made by Janice Paine Dawes, Illinois
1997
74 x 86 inches
Cotton; machine pieced, hand appliquéd, and machine quilted
Reproduction of a quilt with a Hewson Printworks central panel (made circa 1800)
*Collection of Robert Tanis, photo by Brenda Tanis*

The strawberry appliqué quilt was also made from a pattern she found in a magazine. Ginger still has it, and she now also makes quilts.

It was the early 1990s before Janice thought she would try to make another quilt. At the time, she was part of a cooperative gift shop, Keepsake Cottage in Charleston, Illinois, which sold handmade items. This time she was truly hooked, so she began creating small projects to sell in the shop. The shop was sold and the concept changed, though, so Janice had to find a new job.

In 1994, when Janice's husband, Ron, had multiple bypass surgery, they decided to make some changes in their lives. They sold their large Victorian home with an acre of land to move into something smaller and more manageable for him. Janice was working at the time as the finance and insurance manager at a car dealership, but she missed working with her hands. There was no place to work in their new condo, so she rented a small, empty shotgun storefront for a workroom. To help pay the rent, she decided to sell "a few quilt supplies." As she was moving in, the first person to walk through the door squealed, "Look! Fat Quarters! It's true! It's really going to be a quilt shop." And so Bears Paw Drygoods in Mattoon, Illinois, was born.

Within three months, the space was too small, so the store moved to an old carriage house behind a friend's antique store. The store went from a 300-square-foot space to a 1,500-square-foot space with two floors. Janice started giving lessons, and within a few months she was teaching quilt classes nearly every day of the week. "The monster was born," she says. She soon realized that owning a quilt shop was not what her heart desired. She needed to get back to her original intention, which was to create, so she sold the shop. Ron converted half of their garage into a workspace for her. She started making and selling bed quilts along with making hooked rugs and kits.

Meanwhile, Janice had been juried into the Illinois Artisan Program. The Illinois Artisan Program requires that artists must live and work within the state, and their craftwork must then be reviewed and accepted by a jury panel sponsored by the program. Her wares were selling well, so applying to *Early American Home* magazine's (now *Early American Life*) America's Top 200 Craftsman contest, which showcased historical craft, seemed like the next logical step for her. She submitted close ups of a small whole cloth quilted wall hanging and an Amish Whisper quilt to showcase her quilting stitch. Three months later, when she walked inside with the envelope that contained the judges' response, she announced to her husband, "I got my rejection," and was speechless when she opened the letter to discover this was not the case. Not long after she was featured in the magazine, she got a call for a commission. She would need to reproduce an antique quilt; was she interested?

Robert Tanis, director of the Harvard Medical School Department of Genetics, owned a 1750s historical home in Whitinsville, Massachusetts, which served as the starting point for tours to raise money for the Northbridge Historical Society. He had begun to fill the house with artisan-made wares that reflected the time period in which it was built. To accomplish this mission, he had put together a multiple-year plan, and he had gotten to the point at which he needed a quilt for his rope bed.

Says Robert:

After thinking about my quilt requirement for a few weeks, during the spring of 1997, I decided that the two most important features were that it be a working quilt—would not be displayed; no need to pamper and that it properly depict the character of quilts made in the 1750s. At about the time I felt ready to proceed, I unexpectedly came across an important book detailing the history of American quilting, *The American Quilt: A History of Cloth and Comfort 1750–1950* by Roderick Kiracofe [Clarkson Potter Publishers, 1993]. Read it cover to cover with an open mind, learning about early fabric sources, [about] dyes used to color the patterns, and about block printing. Also gained a deep appreciation of how important quilting was to our female early ancestors as a means of artistic expression. Read it a second time specifically searching for examples I felt represented the proper historical motif I sought. There was only one historical quilt that seemed to work, but it was a beauty. The original hung in an upscale antiques store [America Hurrah closed its doors after 30 years in business in 2000] in Manhattan, priced at six figures and in the process of being sold. I called. Never was able to view it.

Robert had interviewed both quiltmakers who had been selected for America's Top 200 Craftsman, but felt a special connection with Janice. He selected her over protests from friends that she was charging too much. It was decided that Janice would recreate the circa 1800, 74-inch by 86-inch Variable Star and Nine Patch quilt with a Hewson Printworks central panel that was showcased in Roderick Kiracofe's book. Since no pattern existed, she would have to draft one.

Finding reproduction fabrics in 1997 was also not an easy task. Janice spent a considerable amount of time searching across the United States for fabric to reproduce the quilt. First, she would send for swatches of quilting cottons and drapery cottons to find acceptable matches, and then she would discuss the selections with Robert before purchasing them.

Nor could she find any Hewson Printworks panels available. John Hewson was born in 1744 in England, was trained as a printer of calico fabrics, and had worked for a leading textile printer near London. In 1774, he opened a calico printing factory in Philadelphia. According to Dr. Kimberly Wulfert, a textile historian, Hewson's textiles were unmatched in America. He is still considered one of the finest craftsmen in textile printing. Martha Washington is said to have visited him and become his patron. Fewer than thirty examples of Hewson's printed fabric in quilts are known to exist today.

The central medallion would present its own problems. For this central panel, Janice started with a piece of natural muslin and built the medallion piece by piece to look as close to the original as possible. Because she could not find fabric with the same bird on it to broderie perse (a method in which printed fabrics are appliquéd onto a background fabric), she chose a bird in the same colorations as the original and improvised for the same look. Robert and Janice made the decision that the color and placement were more important than an exact reproduction of the medallion. For instance, in the original medallion, the right butterfly on the flower sprigs has its antennae up and the left butterfly has its antennae down, and this is not true of the reproduction. Again, it was more important that the positive and negative space in the medallion be as exact as possible to carry through with the look of the original. They also made the decision not to use any colored inks for detailing because it was important to Robert that the final quilt be washable, since he planned to use it to sleep under. Again, they decided to err on the side of caution, believing that colored and India inks might not be permanent.

The quilt was entirely pieced on a vintage portable 1950 Singer Featherweight sewing machine that Janice refers to as her "twin" since they were both born the same year. When it came time to quilt the project, Robert was given the option of hand or heirloom machine quilting. Heirloom machine quilting techniques produce stitching that looks like it was done by hand, so he chose heirloom machine quilting because he intended to use the quilt and wanted to be able to launder it without fear of damage. For the heirloom machine quilting, Janice used her grandmother's 1928 Singer sewing machine.

Janice is not sure of the exact amount of time the quilt took to complete, but her guess is that it was at least six months of intense work. However, after she finished this large commission, she took some real mental down time. This project was so intense for such a long time that she was not really certain she wanted to do that kind of work again for the rest of her life. "It was very hard to take those last hand stitches on the binding and turn it over to someone else. There was so much of my soul in the quilt that it was really almost like a death to be parted from it. It was shortly after that when I quit quilting altogether."

She did attend all the art and fine craft shows she had scheduled for the year. She used the inventory she had and did not add to it with any new quilts. Then she went back to college. After graduating in 2000, Janice sold her stash and any remaining small quilts and moved to Sarasota, Florida. It was not until she moved to Arkansas in 2005 that she decided it was time to get back to making quilts.

Diagnosed with rheumatoid arthritis, she knew she needed to use her hands so that they would not become crippled. She had already endured surgery on three knuckles to free them up and did not want to go through that again. Because she knew how to do heirloom free-motion quilting, she would not be dependent on holding a hoop or take months to complete something by hand, so quilting became her therapy. It was also about this time, while visiting her daughter in Houston, Texas, that she saw her first issue of *Quilting Arts* magazine. "I was instantly in love. There were other people out there who wanted to play with fabric and thread like me! I was hooked on this style of no rules/anything goes, because I don't do rules well. As time has gone by, I have realized that I need to use the traditional quilting skills I taught myself to be successful at art quilting."

Neither Janice nor Robert is sure why they did not keep in touch. In late 2010, Robert decided to see if he could reconnect with Janice, which he successfully did by using the Internet. It was important to him to share with her that the quilt had been used, though never abused. "The quilt was a treasure and constant source of enjoyment," Robert said. When he shared that his plans were to eventually pass the quilt to his daughter, Janice got tears in her eyes. ✑

# HOW HARD COULD IT BE?

Everyone gathered at Robert's house before going to the movies. Barbara Burnham suddenly had a migraine headache, so Robert suggested she take a nap on the sofa. He covered her gently with a quilt made by his grandmother. While attempting to rest, she started looking closely at the quilt. She realized that the seams between all the colorful little hexagons were all stitched by hand, and the quilting was done by hand, too. She had never seen a hand-stitched quilt before and was totally captivated. *Forget the migraine! I have to learn to do this!* she thought.

She enrolled in an evening class at the local high school. At the time, she didn't know the right tools to bring, and the teacher, Pat Litz, laughed at her crewel needle and said, "That's not a needle, that's a crowbar!" Barbara did not give up and

*Pine Tree and Victory*
Made by Anna "Kunie" Kunigunda Kromeke, Baltimore, Maryland
Circa 1940
79½ x 86¾ inches
Cotton; machine pieced and machine quilted
Collection of Barbara Burnham, photo by John Armentout

went on to take more classes. She still has the sampler quilt she created in her first class.

Her mother (Anna Elizabeth Wagner, known by all as Betty) had been impressed when Barbara began making quilts. Betty had made clothes for the whole family, even a tiny Barbie wedding dress, but she had never made quilts. However, Betty did teach Barbara how to sew. Betty's mother (Anna Kunigunda Kromeke, known as Kunie) had died in November 1973 at the age of eighty-three. After discovering Barbara's passion for quilts, Betty thought it only fitting for her to have the one and only quilt that her grandmother had made.

Kunie had taught Barbara how to embroider when she was five. "And she taught me patience. [Since I was an] active child, she gave me a bunch of strings and told me to tie them all up into knots, as many knots as I could. When that was done, she said, 'Now, don't get up out of that chair until you untie them all.' I only fell for that once, but today I can untie anything."

Barbara remembers attending meetings of the Pine Tree Club with her mother, grandmother, and sister in the mid-1950s, and she especially remembers her Aunt Rose playing the grand piano, but she does not remember ever seeing her grandmother's quilt. The Pine Tree Club met on Sunday afternoons in the fellowship hall of St. Paul's Protestant Episcopal Church, more commonly called Old St. Paul's Church today, on North Charles Street in Baltimore, Maryland. Its members were mostly working women who gathered for networking, socializing, and fund-raising. Kunie held a management position in the laundry at St. Agnes Hospital in Baltimore at the time.

During the 1940s, the group raised funds to help military families. A USO club, known as the Charles Street Club, opened across the street from the church on March 15, 1942. The USO—United Services Organization, Inc.—was founded in 1941 in response to a request from President Franklin D. Roosevelt to provide morale and recreation services to U.S. military personnel. It was a private nonprofit organization. The Pine Tree Club helped with dances and other events at the USO for officers and soldiers on leave.

The Charles Street Club was one of seven white servicemen USO clubs throughout Baltimore. Director George Proffit threw away the key to the building "so that the door would always be open for men in uniform." It was used by 40,000 men monthly. Dancing was the most popular activity and drew soldiers from camps throughout Virginia and as far away as North Carolina. Dancing was also important because it built morale "without which no wars were ever won," according to writer Chrystelle Trump Bonds.

*She wasn't a quiltmaker, but she had sewn all her life, so she thought,* How hard could it be?

On the agenda for the club's meeting that particular day was to decide on a new fundraiser. Kunie suggested and the group voted to make a quilt and sell chances to win it. The idea was met with excitement and support. Since Kunie had made the suggestion, she was also expected to make the quilt. She wasn't a quiltmaker, but she had sewn all her life, so she thought, *How hard could it be?* Members donated their nicest house dresses, and one member even donated a set of Nile green bed sheets to use in the quilt. It was decided that, since it was the Pine Tree Club, it was only fitting that the quilt should be made up of Pine Tree blocks. And since they were raising money for military families, it was agreed that alternating blocks would have a *V* for victory.

Dresses were cut up and pieced to form the backgrounds for the simple Pine Tree and V blocks. More calico squares were cut to make the backing. The Nile green sheet was used for Vs, pine trees, sashings, borders on two sides, and the filling inside. All went well until the time came for the actual quilting, sewing the layers together. Betty remembers what occurred next was a lot of struggling, pulling, and pushing, along with several choice words, as her mother tried to sew the layers together on her sewing machine. Her quilting was not straight, but she managed to get it done.

Raffle tickets were printed. Members of the club took turns selling tickets at the USO and to family and friends. There was excitement in the air the day of the drawing. As the president of the organization pulled out the winning ticket, the room got quiet. "And the winner is—Kunie Kromeke." No one remembers if Kunie was thrilled or embarrassed by her win or even if she was the one who purchased the winning ticket.

The *Pine Tree and Victory* quilt has held together over the years, been used and loved, with only a few repairs. Barbara used it for a while until she realized it would not stand up to heavy use, so now it is a cherished part of her vintage collection, which began with her first quilt purchase at a flea market in the 1980s. In addition to collecting, Barbara is a charter member of the Baltimore Album Society and competes in national quilt shows.

Barbara's quilt *M.E.C. Remembered* won second place in the Longarm/Midarm Machine Quilted category at the American Quilter's Society show in Paducah, Kentucky, in 2010. It was professionally longarm quilted by Marty Vint. Barbara provided all the quilting designs. The red and green album-style quilt is a reproduction of a quilt dated 1848 and marked *M.E.C.*, which Barbara found in 1999 at a Chinese antique shop in Virginia Beach, Virginia. The quilt had come from an estate sale. The shop's owner did not speak English, so Barbara had to hire an interpreter to make the deal to purchase it, but she had to have the quilt.

"Thanks to Mom and Grandma, I can sew anything, including quilts that win national awards. Both are gone now, but they would be very proud!" says Barbara Burnham. ✺

# JOE THE QUILTER

In the summer of 1979, at the age of twenty-six, Joe Cunningham returned to Flint, Michigan, his hometown, after his first year of college. Joe had started playing guitar and drums at an early age and began playing music professionally in high school. He was home just for the summer, during which he meant to write the lyrics for a friend's album, and fully intended to return to Colorado to finish college. He got a call from Gwen Marston, who had been told that Joe could accompany her on guitar at some concerts she had booked. When he was at Gwen's house for rehearsal, Joe noticed some boxes full of quilts. Gwen had received a $5,000 grant to document the collection of quilt historian Mary Schafer. She shared that she was really enjoying the documentation itself, but was dreading the writing of the catalog.

"I could do the writing for you," he offered.

---

*Snake in the Garden*
Made by Joe Cunningham, California
2000
73 x 73 inches
Cotton; hand appliquéd, machine pieced, and hand quilted
Inspired by Joseph Hedley, known as "Joe the Quilter"
*Collection of Joe Cunningham, photo by Joe Cunningham*

"Well, you would have to know something about quilts and quilt history," Gwen replied.

Joe fell for her and for quilts at the same time. When he met Mary Schafer, he says, "I fell for her, too." One night Gwen came over to his apartment with a small Drunkard's Path quilt top in a hoop and said, "I'm sick of reading all this stuff by people who never made a quilt in their lives. If you are going to write this catalog, you should know how to quilt." She handed him a big thimble and a tiny needle and showed him a rocking stitch that she had learned from Mennonite quiltmakers.

*Joe fell for Gwen and for quilts at the same time.*

By the time he was done with that crib quilt, his stitches were good enough for him to sit at the frame and quilt on Gwen's quilts with her. Mary was so thrilled that a young man was interested in quilts that she offered to teach him everything she knew on the subject. He decided to forget college and give himself "a college education in quilts."

He began by studying quilt history. That first summer, while reading Averil Colby's book *Quilting* (Charles Scribner's Sons, 1972), he discovered the story of Joseph Hedley—Joe the Quilter. He found a little more about Joe in a Xerox copy of a 1954 book by Mavis Fitzrandolph, *Traditional Quilting: Its Story and Its Practice* (Batsford, London).

Joseph Hedley was born in 1750 in England. He started out as a tailor, but for some unknown reason stopped being a tailor and became a professional quiltmaker. He was poor after having taken care of an invalid wife who had died, and he was on town relief. During his lifetime, however, his talent and fame grew until his quilts were in great demand. He retired alone to a small thatched cottage on Homer's Lane near Warden, Northumberland, and his story could have ended there, but it did not. He was brutally murdered sometime between January 3 and 7, 1826. No one was ever charged with his murder, but the shocking circumstances of his death led to much publicity. Only a few verified quilts made by Joe exist today, including a hand quilted whole cloth quilt in the Bowes Museum in northeast England.

A couple of months after learning about Joe the Quilter, Joe Cunningham decided that he would become a professional quiltmaker. He learned the techniques and absorbed Mary Schafer's concept of the quilt tradition and his place in it. "Even though it was not exactly the life I had pictured, I decided that it was not every day one had the opportunity to study with one of the world's great anythings, and that I should take it seriously," he says.

Throughout the 1980s, he and Gwen wrote a how-to column for the now-defunct magazine *Ladies Circle Patchwork Quilts*. They collaborated on eight books, including the biography *Mary Schafer and Her Quilts* for Michigan State University Museum Press and books for Dover Publications and for the American Quilter's Society, as well as more than sixty articles. They also made a series of videos and started the Beaver Island Quilt Retreat at their home studio on Beaver Island, in the middle of Lake Michigan.

Gwen and Joe also attended the annual quilt show at the most exclusive shopping mall in Detroit, the Somerset Mall, organized and promoted by Merry Silber. On impulse, Joe introduced himself to Merry, letting her know that he and Gwen were teaching and that they were available should she ever need teachers for the show on short notice. Sure enough, the next year, one of Merry's teachers cancelled at the last minute, so she called them to fill in. During the show, Merry introduced them to her daughter, Julie Silber, who had come from San Francisco to give her annual lecture at the show. The moment Julie and Joe met, there was a connection, and they became close friends. "We were like brother and sister without the fighting," says Joe.

When Joe and Gwen split in 1991, he moved to New York City to be the music director for a theater company, then to Warren, Vermont, to host a radio show. In 1993, after the radio show failed, he did commercial music projects. Julie called and asked him to write the brochures for her new business, The Quilt Complex, and also to help her organize and write the materials for a series of quilt shows she had booked in Sweden, Germany, and Japan. Altogether, she hired him for five months, starting December 1. "After one long winter in Vermont, I was thrilled to be going to San Francisco for the winter," Joe says.

Josh, a friend, asked Joe if he knew anyone in San Francisco. He said, "You have to call my cousin, Carol LeMaitre. She works at a music school, and she will introduce you to all the musicians in town." Joe ended up marrying her, staying in San Francisco, and starting a family. They have two sons. He also started making quilts again in 1994.

In 2000, he discovered Janet Rae's book *Quilts of the British Isles* (Dutton Books, 1987), which again featured the story of

Joseph Hedley's life and unsolved murder, as well as the lyrics to "The Ballad of Joe the Quilter." Joe realized that writing the music for an English ballad would be no problem, and he could take his guitar with him on quilt engagements. It would "combine these two seemingly irreconcilable parts of my life," he says. But when he read the lyrics, he hated them. They were all about how "old Joe" died instead of being about his life, so Joe decided to write his own "Ballad of Joe the Quilter."

Joe Cunningham's version told the story of the first part of Joe Hedley's life, up to the end of his apprenticeship and through the opening of his tailor shop. Julie liked it and said, "What happens next?" Suddenly, an ambitious idea sprang to life in his mind. He would write a series of six songs to tell the story of Joe's life, and when the story reached the point where the title character started making quilts, Joe would make the quilts. "This would give me a reason to make quilts like I had long pictured, wholly original quilts making artistic statements, but made with all the aesthetic materials of old quilts."

Joe's quilt *Blue and White* was made in 2001 to experiment with the idea of making freehand versions of classic patterns. In the musical, this is also called *Joe Hedley's First Quilt*.

*Bird Flees the Thorns*, made in 2002, is the second quilt Joe makes. It is a mourning quilt for his late wife and includes freehand broderie perse and quilting designs.

*Snake in the Garden* is based on a quilt that Joe Hedley supposedly created. It appears midway through the musical, when Joe suffers a sort of midlife crisis, and the joy begins to leak out of his work and life. Eventually, Joe decides to make a masterpiece quilt on the subject of the Garden of Eden. The quilt is similar to the medallions of the period, which often included a central image of a tree of life, with images from the Garden of Eden like birds and flowers. Joe decides to make his on the same theme, but with the snake in the middle. He thinks that if he makes this masterpiece quilt full of symbolism and so artfully composed, people will understand that he has changed what quilts are capable of, that they will understand that everything is different now, that quilts could be used to convey complex ideas. Of course, what happens is that no one understands it as anything other than a nice quilt, but it helps him get out of his funk.

*The Time to Quilt* was made in 2003. One of two quilts made to illustrate how Joe made all kinds of quilts in his quest to make one for everyone in his village, it has different wool fabrics in the center and a cotton border.

*Straw into Gold* was made in 2004. It was made later in Joe Hedley's career—in the musical—to represent a sort of crazy scrap quilt. "I was, once again, trying to use traditional materials for my own purposes. My idea was to create an anti-medallion, with nothing in the middle and a series of borders that crash into it," explains Joe Cunningham.

*Joe Hedley's Last Quilt* was made in 2003 out of wool. Joe says, "I stole the clashing red and blue color scheme from a quilt in Marsha MacDowell's book *African American Quiltmaking in Michigan* [Michigan State University Press, 1998]. It was meant to evoke a sort of calm authority, supposedly made in Joe's eightieth year to imitate the lights in the windows of his village at night. I did fancy freehand feather quilting, just to see if I could do it."

In 2001, Joe Cunningham began performing his musical *Joe the Quilter* all across the United States as he worked on the quilts. A 2007 performance in Modesto, California, was recorded and made available on DVD.

Nearly two hundred years after his life, Joseph Hedley, known as Joe the Quilter, inspired another Joe to become a professional quiltmaker. To honor his mentor, Joe Cunningham not only wrote a musical and made quilts, but he has adopted the name Joe the Quilter. ✍

# MARY MOON,
# WHO WERE YOU?

W hile Jack Lindsey is an antiques dealer and owner of Doodletown Antiques in Ancram, New York, he also has a passion for preserving the history of his adopted town and is an enthusiastic and dedicated volunteer with the Ancram Preservation Group. Founded in the early 1740s, Ancram began as a land grant given to the Livingston family. It was originally called Livingston Forge after the iron forge on the Hudson River that played a significant role in the American Revolution. Founded in September 2000, the Ancram Preservation Group has been instrumental in saving and preserving the 1860s-era Simmons General Store in the center of town, and has earmarked several other structures in town for preservation efforts.

Jack put out the word that he was looking for textiles with a connection to Columbia County, New York, or Ancram,

---

**Album quilt**
Made by Mary Moon (1837–1859), Ancram, New York
1856
87 x 95 inches
Cotton; hand pieced, hand appliquéd, embroidered, and hand quilted
*Collection of the Ancram Preservation Group, photo by B. Docktor Photography*

specifically. His friends have always been amazed with his great radar for unearthing unique finds. As his friend Lynne Perrella drove over to Jack's house one June day in 2010, she had no way of knowing that this visit would become the "flashpoint" for a new body of work. It would also deepen her appreciation for the history of this rural town in the Hudson River Valley, which she had moved to from Manhattan in 1988, having spent weekends in the area and fallen in love with it.

Lynne graduated from the Art Institute of Pittsburgh with a certification in fashion illustration. After moving to New York City in 1967, she began her career as a commercial artist and in 1970 cofounded Perella Design, Inc. with her husband, John. For more than thirty years, she worked as an illustrator and designer, specializing in corporate communications, advertising, and promotion. Her focus now is on paper. She is a mixed media artist, author, and workshop instructor. She travels around the world sharing her talent and passion.

Jack had invited her to see his latest find—"an extra-special quilt." Lynne anticipated seeing an oddball crazy quilt. Instead, she was rewarded with a perfectly preserved red and white album quilt replete with the embroidered names of families who lived and worked in Ancram during the mid-1850s. Best of all, the maker had signed and dated her work: *Mary Moon, 1856.* Lynne had to know more.

Jack had learned about the quilt, along with a simpler damaged quilt possibly by the same maker, from an antiques dealer in Virginia who had acquired them from a member of the Mary Moon Rockefeller family. The second quilt had numerous tears and stains and had a much simpler pattern. It is not clear why they had descended together, but regardless, the simpler quilt was in bad shape. Perhaps the fancier quilt, which was more intricate and detailed, was more cherished, and used less. At any rate, when Jack realized that the quilt in excellent condition was embroidered with the names of local families and dated, he felt it was something that should be acquired on behalf of the town, and he worked with the Ancram Preservation Group to make that happen.

The following week, Lynne made an appointment with Clara Van Tassel, the town's second-generation historian. (She had followed in the footsteps of her late mother.) The state of New York requires that every town have a town historian, responsible for preserving the past, including town documents, buildings, and artifacts. Historians are often instrumental in helping towns store historical items so that they may be preserved for posterity.

Clara was able to provide Lynne with some information. It was evident that Mary Moon had completed the quilt in her nineteenth year, the same year she married a local farmer named Albert Rockefeller. Lynne imagined that the completed quilt might have been unveiled at an engagement party or church supper surrounded by family and friends. "I envisioned the young bride carefully folding the quilt, and placing it in a sturdy blanket chest that would travel with them by horse and wagon to their first home," says Lynne.

No one knows much about Mary and Albert, except that they were married only three short years and had two children. Mary died at the age of twenty-two. No records exist to explain the cause of death, but Lynne and Clara speculate that it might have been due to complications during childbirth. After Mary's death, Albert remarried and several of his children remained in the Ancram area until the 1940s. They were local merchants and maintained small shops in town. Albert died in 1922.

Without any actual details about Mary and how, where, or why she created her quilt, Lynne decided to learn more about her town's history during Mary's brief lifetime. With Clara's help, Lynne explored mountains of old correspondence, farm ledgers, newspapers, programs from local theatrical performances, accounts of church suppers, town meetings, and—best of all—endless vintage photographs of the era. Many of the photographs had been studiously identified and labeled, but not all. Occasionally Lynne would inquire about a particularly captivating photograph, and Clara would simply smile and reply, "An Ancram resident. We're just not sure who they were, but they definitely lived here." Clara is a natural storyteller who enjoys sharing her passion for Ancram, past and present, and Lynne found Clara's lifelong interest in local history infectious. It was not long before Lynne was working on a series of new collages.

"As a collage artist, I love arranging scraps and bringing some sense of harmony and richness to the layers," Lynne says. "As I began this series, I realized that quilting is a lot like collage. Both art forms are autobiographical and personal and rely on using existing found materials to create something new."

The use of old ephemera was not new to Lynne; however, working with authenticated historical images was something completely new to her. "I felt I was caretaking the enduring traditions of the small rural hamlet I love, and I wanted to bring my best efforts to the task. Clara's stories always have an undercurrent of telltale detail and place names, so I wanted my collages to reflect not only the town of people, but the places where they lived and worked." Also, in each of the 11 inch by 14-inch collages (four so far), Lynne has included visual elements of Mary's quilt, not only as a continuing motif throughout the series, but also to acknowledge the source of her inspiration.

While working on her collage *Life Lessons*, which has photographs of long-ago schoolchildren posing outside a one-room schoolhouse with their teacher standing close by, Lynne was having a tough time deciding which photograph to use because she had so many good choices. Finally, Clara pointed to one little girl with a serious face, a ruffled dress, and high-top shoes, saying, "That girl was my mother." For

*"I felt I was caretaking the enduring traditions of the small rural hamlet I love."*

Lynne, the stories Clara shared about the many one-room schoolhouses struck a deep chord within her and evoked rural America at its best.

Apparently, Ancram was the home of many one-room schoolhouses. The schools would be built wherever there was a concentration of young children and farm families. Thanks to Clara's insights, Lynne has driven around and located many of the former schoolhouses. Some of them were houses she has driven by every day, never realizing that their former purpose was to serve as a school. Others are long-abandoned wooden buildings engulfed in heavy shrubs and trees. Often, these are only visible during winter because they are so hidden by overgrowth. "I get the feeling that these buildings are being gradually 'reclaimed' by the land," says Lynne. In her photo archives, Clara has dozens of photos of the schoolhouses and the children. "It's great fun to see some little scamp in short pants, in the second row of one of the photos, and realize he is now the old gent enjoying his morning coffee at the deli," Lynne adds.

*Always and Ever* features the old stone bridge that still spans the Roeliff Jansen Kill, the narrow waterway that rushes through the town and travels to the Hudson River. The winter view of Ancram is relatively unchanged from days past. Lynne used lots of original vintage elements from her own collection as well as digital prints of photographs from Clara's archive to complete this project.

*Strong Hold* depicts structures of the town, most long gone, woven into the background. The stalwart hardworking men pictured in it, whether farmers or railroad workers, have a strong look of dependability. Lynne wanted the completed collage to have the vibe of an old, well-worn blue work shirt.

A penciled inscription on the back of a photograph, *Sunday Picnic*, inspired the composition and title for Lynne's fourth collage. "Rich with details, the photo provided lots of visual clues, so I could easily imagine everyone packing up the wagons on an early fall day and heading for a favorite picnic spot with a view of the Berkshires. I envisioned them opening the lunch baskets, and after sharing their meal, each person indulged in some afternoon reverie, whether reading, embroidery, smoking a pipe, or napping," says Lynne.

Lynne plans to continue creating art in this series until the subject matter no longer interests her. Three of the collages were on display at Ancram Community Day festivities during the summer of 2010, and images of the collages were made into blank note cards, along with other historical memorabilia and an image of the quilt, and sold to raise funds for the local playground. Lynne is also a "helper" with the Ancram Preservation Group.

Mary Moon's quilt has been carefully restored by an expert in vintage textiles and framed. It will hang in the Town Hall, a gift from the Ancram Preservation Group, as visible evidence of shared history. Everyone thinks Mary would be pleased.

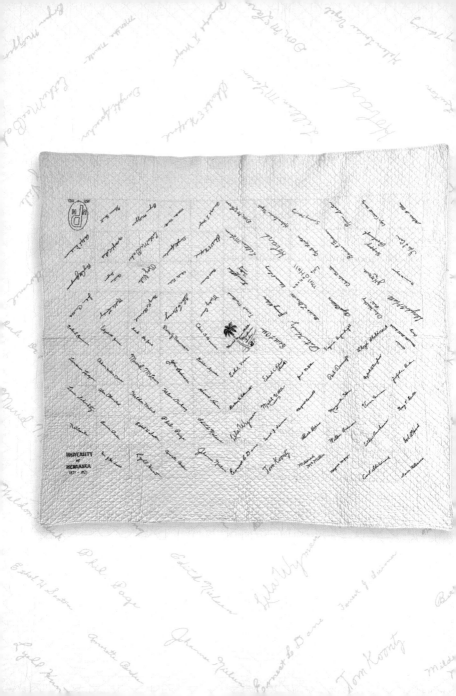

# IN HONOR OF HARRIET

The red and white quilt with one hundred signatures was discovered among the donations for the Mendocino Presbyterian Church's 1998 Rummage-O-Rama. The annual sale was to raise money for the youth group's annual summer mission trip. One corner of the quilt had a large *P* centered between a *u* and *n* and *1871–1921* embroidered on it. Another corner block had *University of Nebraska 1871–1921* stitched on it. The center contained the name *Harriet Wyman Wilder, Madura, India,* and a palm tree embroidered on the square. William L. Mangrum, pastor of the church, decided it was a memory quilt commemorating the fiftieth anniversary of the university (1871–1921). He mailed it from his California church to the alumni office at the University of Nebraska–Omaha. The alumni office forwarded it to the University of Nebraska–Lincoln Alumni Association.

---

**Signature quilt**
Maker unknown (eighty signatures connected to the UNL-Palladian Literary Society, Lincoln, Nebraska)
Circa 1921
69 x 74 inches
Cotton; hand and machine pieced, embroidered, and hand quilted
*Courtesy of the International Quilt Study Center and Museum, University of Nebraska–Lincoln. (1998.004.0001)*

Lee Denker of the Alumni Association in turn gave it to the International Quilt Study Center and Museum (IQSC) in Lincoln, Nebraska.

By strange luck, when volunteers were discussing a logo on the quilt that simply read "UNP," one of the volunteers mentioned that she had just read something about the Palladian Society.

On September 29, 1871, twenty boys and five girls met and formed the Palladian Literary Society at the University of Nebraska. This is also the same year the university began conducting classes. *Palladian* is derived from Latin and means "pertaining to wisdom, knowledge, or study." When searching for information on the names found on the quilt, researchers discovered that it did indeed reference members of the Palladian Literary Society of the early 1920s. The club's historian shared that in many ways this club was a glorified dating service, as each male member was required to take a new date to each function. "The guys simply had to write their names next to a gal's on the club's slate, the gal sent a thank-you note, and the date was set," according to the historian. The club was disbanded in 1969 due to the university's move to a fraternity/sorority system.

According to the *Palladian Quarter Centennial History*, page 165, "The aims of the society are: to promote facility in public speaking and general literary work, to give the students the social culture and recreation which is so much needed, and to foster the spirit of democracy. . . . Our societies are distinguished from most college literary societies by three characteristics. First, they are co-educational; second, they are 'barbarian,' having found in their A B C years that the secret college fraternities caused a division among society workers, which was simply suicidal to harmonious action and eventually death to the society; third, they are alive."

The date of 1921 refers to the Palladian's semi-centennial celebration organized by the Palladian Alumni Association. Through the examination of UNL yearbooks, it was discovered that Harriet Wyman Wilder was a missionary who did indeed spend time in Madura, India, working as an assistant principal and instructor at a girls' school. It was also discovered that two of the individuals who had signed their names to the small squares of muslin in the quilt were still living.

The quilt was displayed for the first time in an exhibition titled *Scarlet and Cream* at the International Quilt Study Center and Museum June 10–September 2, 2002 (Scarlet and cream are the colors for the University of Nebraska.) The exhibition celebrated the fifth anniversary of the Quilt Center's founding. The description of the quilt read:

Palladian Signature Quilt—This red and white signature quilt offers a glimpse into the history of the University of Nebraska Through research in the University of Nebraska Lincoln archives, we discovered that many of the names embroidered on the redwork signature quilt represent members of the Palladian Society, a UNL literary organization. The group was founded the same year as the University began classes—1871. The quilt commemorates the 50th anniversary of the organization and the University, as well as the beginning of a mission to India for a society member, Harriet Wyman Wilder, in 1921.

## CHAPTER TWENTY-FOUR

Harriet's name is embroidered in the center block of the quilt,
accompanied by a palm tree in outline embroidery and the
location Madura, India.

It was believed that the quilt was either made by or for
Harriet in Lincoln, Nebraska, and/or Madura, India, circa
1920–1930. The two surviving women who had signed the quilt
were invited to attend a special lecture on the Palladian Society
given by Mary Ellen Ducey, UNL special collections librarian
and archivist, on August 27, 2002. Margaret McGregor was
able to attend and had her photograph taken with the quilt.
Unfortunately, neither woman remembered signing a square
nor why the quilt was made.

In August 2007, Carolyn Ducey, curator of collections
at the International Quilt Study Center and Museum, asked
volunteer Joan Laughlin to do further research on the quilt.
Joan began her research of the hundred names by using U.S.
census records from 1920 and 1930. Although she did not learn
more about Harriet Wyman Wilder, she did discover basic
information about most of the people who signed the quilt
blocks. For some of the people, membership in the Palladian
Society could be confirmed from newspaper articles dating
from 1918 to the late 1950s. A very active Palladian Alumni
group, called PALs ("Pal" was what members called each other),
met socially and held a centennial reunion in 1974. Some were
faculty members, including Harriet, who was also an honorary
member of the society.

Several of those who were not established as members
were the spouses of members or those who had other family

(children) who held membership in the Palladian Literary Society. Joan also discovered that some of the people had connections with Harriet through organizations like the Girl Scouts, as fellow faculty members, and in other ways. Marriages between some of the signers were discovered, and some signers may have shared employment with others (emphasis for the research was on employment shared with Harriet). For some, church-related commonalities were found. For six persons, Roy Biele, John Cestek, Ralph Dickinson, J. H. McMillin, Mildred McMillin, and Sidney Thirding, little or no information was uncovered.

A real breakthrough came when Joan found the names of the children of Harriet and Dr. Edward Wilder. The initial source of this information was the manifest of the *Queen Mary*, the boat the family used to travel to India on June 6, 1938. Knowing the identities of the four sons (Charles, John, David, and Donald) enabled Joan to search online for them, using search engines and online phone directories. She was successful in locating three of the sons, and wrote to them in November 2007. The letter generated a rich and fruitful e-mail exchange that led to several important conclusions: that the quilt had never gone to India, that the sons had never seen the quilt, and that the family was very interested in the quilt's story.

Granddaughter Emily Van Dalen wrote:

Just wanted to write and thank you for all the work you have done in researching the Palladian quilt made for my Grandmother Wilder. A few months ago I was "googling" the web with her name just to see what might come up and discovered that there was a quilt at the Univ. of Nebraska that was somehow related to her. I mentioned this at our Wilder Thanksgiving get-together last week (all four brothers and families get together every Thanksgiving at David Wilder's home in Lewisburg, PA . . . we Wilders have a strong sense of family and heritage). What an amazing thing that your email to my Uncle Don coincided with that remark . . . we have all been in a flurry of emails ever since.

I grew up in Pakistan where my parents (John & Dorothy Wilder) served for 40 years . . . so I only saw my grandparents occasionally when we went on furlough every 4-6 years. But my memory of Grandmother Wilder is quite clear . . . she was quite an indomitable lady and made an impression on those who knew her even casually. I smiled when I read in your timeline of her activities for women's suffrage . . . because it is so in-character . . . she was strongly opinioned, especially when it came to issues of justice and truth.

I also was thrilled at the mention of her marriage details, for only last week many old family photos were distributed among the grandkids and I ended up with a lovely, yellowed 5 x 8 photo of the wedding group. She is standing with one attendant with a beautiful armful of flowers, a tea-length white gown, and the family wedding veil. Her arm is linked into that of my grandfather and both wear very modest "Mona Lisa"–type smiles on their faces. There are also two male attendants in the photo.

The Wilder sons, grandchildren, and Joan exchanged at least three dozen e-mails, which led to the conclusion that the quilt had not traveled to India and back again as assumed. Among Harriet's sons, John, deceased, had studied in California, but no other family member had lived there. Charles had suggested that it was "made in [his mother's] honor, but never given to her" and that perhaps it "hung in the place where the Palladian Society met."

Joan considered that one of the signers might have lived in California. She found Margaret Cannell, who died on September 10, 2000, in Menlo Park. Menlo Park is 184 miles north of Mendocino, where the quilt was donated for the church's sale. Another person who signed the quilt, Sharlet Wolford, died in August 1983, in Fullerton (southern California). One could theorize that Margaret Cannell was the maker of the quilt and had it in her possession until late in life. It is possible that she was moved to a care facility prior to her death, and that her possessions were distributed to others. She had never married.

While Joan was concentrating on finding out more about Harriet, she came across a book written by her called *A Century in the Madura Mission, South India, 1834–1934* (Vantage Press, 1961). Joan ordered the book from an antique books dealer in Australia. When it arrived, it was autographed in pencil: "To Ruth, Harriet Wyman Wilder." Joan, together with Ph.D. student Jonathan Gregory, compared the signature on the front page of the book to the center block. They could not believe their eyes. Harriet Wyman Wilder had not signed the center block of the quilt.

The questions began again: Who made the quilt? Where had it been since its creation in 1922–1923? How did it end up in Mendocino, California? We may never know. ❧

# EYE OF PANIC

"Imagine the feeling of being on a plane that is going down. That's the same feeling of a panic attack, but with a panic attack, you're the only one feeling it. The plane going down would feel like a relief because it would be real," says Lucinda Bassett, founder of the Midwest Center for Stress and Anxiety, headquartered in Oak Harbor, Ohio. For Linda Edkins Wyatt, "In a panic attack, you have an overwhelming feeling that you are about to die. It comes out of nowhere with little or no warning. I feel like I need to scream, tear off my clothes, and run around the streets naked. I get diarrhea, moderately nauseous, hands shake, hyperventilate, and sweat. It is complete, overwhelming terror and a very claustrophobic feeling."

Linda began having minor panic attacks when she was a child. In her twenties, they seemed to occur when she had too much caffeine, and they could also be triggered by heat. In the 1990s, when both her parents were dying and her husband lost the job that provided the family with income and benefits,

---

*Eye of Panic*
Made by Linda Edkins Wyatt, New York
2010
36 x 36 inches
Pellon and cotton; machine pieced, photo transfer, hand painted, and machine quilted
*Collection of Linda Edkins Wyatt, photo by Jose L. Torres Jr.*

the panic attacks were intense. She tried medication, but it prevented her from sleeping even if she swam laps thirty to forty minutes a day. Her hair started turning green from all the time she was spending in the pool. She was exhausted. She tried therapy. While attempting to figure out the cause of the panic attacks, she even consulted her siblings to see if some kind of trauma had occurred in her childhood that she did not remember. They could not come up with anything. She tried alternative medicine. Nothing seemed to work.

At the time, she was also working five days a week for her husband's small business, *The Medical Herald* (no longer being published). She was driving her daughter, Amanda, back and forth to school through Manhattan traffic twice a day. On Fridays, the family would escape the city by driving 102 miles on the Long Island Expressway to the country. After enjoying a quiet weekend, they would have to drive the 102 miles back to Manhattan either Sunday night or very early Monday morning. Trying to be a superwoman who had it all finally took its toll.

In 1999, the panic attacks had gotten so bad that Linda knew she had to make some big changes. The family decided to move permanently to the eastern tip of Long Island. Between childrearing and business deadlines, art had been pushed to the back burner. (Linda's bachelor's degree is in elementary education with a concentration in art. She also earned an associate of applied science degree in textile design.) Linda decided it was time to incorporate creative activities into her healing process. She painted and collaged. She made jewelry, rolling and baking her own beads. Her mixed-media works combined painting and sewing and incorporated shells and beach glass from the shores of Long Island.

For a few years, her panic attacks subsided. Then, in 2006, they became more frequent and intense again. One hot summer afternoon, Linda was having consecutive panic attacks. Her husband and daughter played soft music and cooled her with ice. Amanda asked if she wanted to draw and brought Linda her bin of crayons and a stack of white paper. Linda began to scribble madly. Quite by accident, she discovered that by directing her pent-up panic energy, she could give the panic a safe way to come out. Additionally, focusing her mind on something other than her symptoms made the attack pass more quickly. She was still drained afterward, but relaxed. Amazingly, she could sleep. She kept scribbling during the attacks in the months that followed. When she questioned her primary care physician about it, he told her that creating art produces serotonin in the body, and that is why the scribbling helped. Serotonin contributes to the feeling of well-being.

> *Linda discovered that focusing her mind on something other than her symptoms made the attack pass more quickly.*

Linda's mom had been a quiltmaker who loved to make Cathedral Window quilts by hand. She had made one for each of her six children, including Linda. She also made Amish-inspired quilts that were machine and hand quilted. Linda made her first quilt in the 1970s in high school from prequilted samples from a salesman's sample book. She also finished a Postage Stamp quilt from the 1940s that someone in the family had started. She collects quilts, too—some of her favorites are a quilt made of printed feedsacks ("falling apart, but still dear to my heart") and a turn-of-the-century crazy quilt that has been handed down through the family. Linda had always loved quilts but had felt that taking on a huge, bed-sized quilt project was beyond her patience level.

However, sewing had always been a part of Linda's life. Like many girls in the 1970s, she made most of her own clothes. When it came time to go to college, she studied textile design at the Fashion Institute of Technology in New York City, and then she worked as a print stylist in the fabric business during the 1980s. It was not until 2007 that she returned to making quilts; only this time, she began creating art quilts. In late 2006, while in a bookstore, she came across an issue of *Quilting Arts* magazine. "I had no idea that art quilting existed, and I thought I had died and gone to heaven when I found the art quilt world and kindred spirits," she says. Art quilting provided her with opportunities to combine all the art techniques that she loved doing.

Her panic attacks come on suddenly and often occur in the middle of the night. Crayons remain her favorite tool. As the panic occurs, Linda reaches first for a black or purple crayon. As she feels more in control, she adds other colors. As an added bonus, she finds the smell of crayons soothing. "There is no intent in the scribbling process other than to keep my hands busy, redirect the panic energy in a safe way, and focus my mind on something other than feeling helpless and frightened."

Linda admits that her scribble drawings are not usually very good. Instead, they are childlike and harsh, but therapeutic nonetheless. For the most part, she did not use them in her work at the start. "It may be that they are just plain ugly or that they remind me of feeling panicky, frantic, and horribly sick." However, eventually, she began to play with her initial scribbles and incorporate them into her quilts. Scanning them into her computer allows her to make adjustments and play around with layout and composition. She experiments with the designs in different sizes and arrangements, even mixing pieces together.

*Eye of Panic* was created in 2010 to celebrate Linda's victory over panic disorder. First she called it *KO* for knockout, since she felt that it marked her last big panic attack, and although the attack was several hours long and difficult, "somehow I knew it would be my last big attack," she shares. The border is composed of alternating squares of fabric. The round, sun-like blocks come from a crayon panic drawing that was later scanned and printed on fabric. The other squares were cut from a large piece of Pellon (a type of interfacing) that she had scribbled on with crayons during a very long, intense attack. She adds:

I did an allover free-motion quilting stitch on it. I didn't know what to do with it, so I just left it hanging on my studio door for a while. Then I decided it would be therapeutic to cut it up, very symbolic, so I did. But then I didn't know what to do with the cut, quilted pieces, so I put them in my UFO [unfinished objects] drawer. After a while, I realized that if I alternated them with another panic design it would look interesting, so I printed the sun-shaped design on heat transfer sheets, ironed them to cotton, cut them to size, and quilted them.

I had done a self-portrait piece called *Mime* that was in Cate Prato's book *Mixed-Media Self-Portraits* [Interweave Press, 2008]. I really liked the way I did the eye in it, so I made a giant one and did a new painting on cloth for the center. I especially liked quilting the eye and used colored threads to accent the eye, then I stitched with lines of thread to accent the eye also. I printed a photo of my own eye and over-painted it with water-soluble oil pastels, fabric markers, and acrylic. The large central eye signifies my newfound strength, health, and well-being. I puttered with different ways to connect the whole thing, and the grommet/chain link seemed right. Somehow cutting it all up and putting it back together with strong metal findings made me feel like I was rebuilding myself after panic, making myself stronger, uniting the whole mind/body/soul with fiber and metal. In creating *Eye of Panic*, I have symbolically cut panic down to size, contained and restrained it, and stitched it shut. I have looked at panic—unafraid—with my giant, unwavering eye, and made it retreat.

*Eye of Panic* hangs proudly in Linda's living room.

Today, Linda does not take any medication. The attacks have dwindled to practically none. If she does start to feel that an attack is coming, she breathes through it. Meditating regularly helps. Of course, she uses the crayon scribbling as needed. "I feel strongly that the scribble technique has helped me a great deal," she says, "and also finding some time to do a little artwork every day calms me and keeps the panic from erupting." For Linda, quilts are full of memories, not just those in the fabric scraps, but her own memories of her mother making quilts. "There is a contentedness in quilting It triggers happy memories of my mother's nightly quilting in the living room while my father watched TV, and memories of him helping her thread the needle when she got older and couldn't see the eye anymore. The act of stitching is also very meditative; both the hum of the electric sewing machine and the repetitiveness of hand stitching are soothing, allowing my mind to wander and clear." ∾

# LEGACY RECLAIMED

The treasure trove from the early 1900s had been boxed and stashed in the third-floor studio for twenty years, but now it was unearthed for the estate sale of Ruby Short McKim. Family members had salvaged some things before the sale began, but many treasures from the McKims' house went off with curious shoppers that day in 1985.

Barbara McKim Frohoff had been married to Ruby's son, Kim McKim, from 1953 until 1970, when they divorced. They had lived above McKim Studios when they were first married, and Barbara had loved her mother-in-law deeply. It was just by chance that she was driving by the studio the day of the sale and realized something was happening. When she entered, she found that the estate sale was over. Odds and ends were scattered here and there. The woman in charge told her, "Take whatever you want. The men are on their way to haul what is left to the trash." Since Barbara had spent a lot of time at the

---

**Oriental Poppy**
Pattern by Ruby Short McKim, quilt made from c. 1930 original kit by Rose Werner,
    Duluth, Minnesota
2011
48 x 30 inches
Cotton; machine-pieced, hand-appliquéd, embroidered, and hand-quilted
*Collection of Merrily McKim Tuohey, photo by Merrily McKim Tuohey*

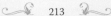

studio, she knew where things were kept. She could not bear to see the work and treasures of her former mother-in-law lost and thrown away.

In the fall of 2005, Barbara and her daughter, Merrily McKim Tuohey, were discussing the wonders of the Internet. Barbara mentioned that she had a "few" of Merrily's grandmother's patterns. "Do you think something could be done with them?"

Merrily always knew her grandmother, Ruby Short McKim, had something to do with quilts, but she never knew the details. She had grown up helping her dad, Kim, around the Kimport Dolls office, and she remembered her grandmother as loving and attentive. She always looked forward to having her turn to spend the night at her grandparents' house. She would stay in her dad's old room with the curtains that her grandmother had made, and her favorite memories include sitting at the game nook in the library with the *McKims at Work* and the *McKims at Play* murals her grandmother had created, learning how to write in cursive. She also loved when her grandmother would read to her from her vast collection of children's books.

And yet, this simple question from her mother would set Merrily on the path to discoveries about her grandmother that even her mother did not know. And over the years, as Barbara gave things to Merrily, she would say, "That's it." However, she always seemed to "come across" something more.

Ruby Short was born in Millersburg, Illinois, in 1891. Her older sister, Cordie, was born in 1881, and her brother, June, in 1884. In 1899, the family moved to Independence, Missouri, into a log cabin riddled with bullet holes from the Civil War. Her father, Morris T. Short, a frontier missionary affiliated with the Reorganized Church of Jesus Christ of Latter-day Saints (now Community of Christ) died in 1901. The family had to live on donations from church members and her mother's job as a librarian with the church.

Ruby's mother, Viola Vernon Short, was a powerful role model. She was an accomplished teacher before marriage, and a strong promoter of children's education. (During those times, women were not allowed to continue being teachers after they married.) Later she even published her own book, *The Lone Relaford*, and traveled around the country promoting it at the same time the McKims were traveling to promote their quilt patterns.

Ruby showed an early interest in drawing, carrying a sketchbook everywhere she went. After graduating from high school in 1910, her uncle sponsored her studies at the New York School of Fine and Applied Arts, now known as Parsons The New School for Design. After she graduated in 1912, she returned to Independence, becoming the Supervisor of Drawing for the Independence School District and a very popular teacher. In 1916, she taught at Manual Training High School in Kansas City, Missouri.

Ruby was chosen as the winner of a contest held by the *Kansas City Star* to design a quilt pattern for children, which would be published in the paper. Her *Quaddy Quiltie* quilt blocks were published in a promotion that was co-copyrighted with the author. This was her first and probably most famous quilt series.

Ruby married Arthur McKim, a public relations businessman, in 1917, and together they planned to market Ruby's art ideas. As a boy, while ice skating, Arthur fell through the ice and injured his hip. His family did not have money for medical treatment, so he was lame for the rest of his life. His family realized that he could not make a living doing labor, so they moved from Denison, Iowa, to Independence, Missouri, so that he could attend high school. They chose Independence because they were also members of the Reorganized Church of Jesus Christ of Latter-day Saints.

Following her dream to inspire others' creativity through her art designs, Ruby stopped only to give birth to Betty, their first child, in 1918. From about 1920 to 1922, the McKims were on the road, building business relationships across the country in order to sell Ruby's quilt patterns and needlework designs, while family members at home took care of Betty. When their second child, Marilyn, was born in 1923, the family told them, "It is time to stay home!" All the traveling paid off, though. In January 1922, Ruby became the children's art editor of a new publication, *Child Life Magazine*. Her work with the magazine, which included quilt patterns and needlework projects for children, would last sixteen years.

Settling down in Independence, Arthur worked for a Kansas City ad agency to support his family, while Ruby taught art in the basement of their house and continued supplying newspapers with new quilt patterns. In 1925, Arthur accepted an advertising job for the Brown Shoe Company, moving the family to St. Louis. Ruby continued her work. In 1927, the church wanted Arthur's help in researching and promoting the truth behind its founding, so they returned to Independence.

In 1928, Ruby and Arthur started McKim Studios, their home-based mail order business. Their *Designs Worth Doing* and *Adventures in Needlecraft* catalogs featured many original patterns as well as smaller quilts from early Americana. McKim Studios offered their patterns, with or without fabric, or the option of purchasing ready-cut quilt kits. The company even offered quilting services, with the quilts completed on frames in the attic.

*Although newspapers initially provided quilt patterns as a service, editors quickly realized that this service meant money.*

Throughout this time, the McKims continued establishing contacts in the publishing world. The relationship with the *Kansas City Star* began in 1916. When the *Star* started publishing quilt pattern series in 1928, Ruby was their designer for the first three years. More than 1,000 quilt patterns were printed in a ready-to-use format from 1928 to 1961 in the *Kansas City Star* and its sister publications, the *Weekly Star* and the *Star Farmer*. Although newspapers initially provided quilt patterns as a service, editors quickly realized that this service meant money, both in increased circulation and through the sale of patterns. Ruby continued designing intermittently for the *Star* and other newspapers around the country until 1935. Eveline Foland took over as the *Star*'s designer.

In the early 1920s, *Women's World* magazine featured Ruby's *Jolly Circus Quilt* and *Betty Blue and Bobby Shaftoe*, familiar nursery characters of the day, in their publication. Ruby's "Adventures in Home Beautifying" column for *Better Homes & Gardens* magazine focused on a different room of the house or craft idea each month. This lasted until 1938, although she wrote under the pen name of Doris Hale the last four years.

In 1931, Ruby published *One Hundred and One Patchwork Patterns*. The book was a compilation of traditional quilt patterns redrawn or reworked by Ruby, with the informative text written by her and possibly Arthur. People were using her book well into the 1970s. It has been reprinted numerous times and remains in print today.

Ruby was one of the only quilt designers to capitalize on the uniquely twentieth-century Art Deco influence for her stylized flower designs. Among the flowers she interpreted in this style were the iris, poppy, and trumpet vine. One of the items Barbara rescued from the estate sale was Ruby's popular *Oriental Poppy* kit, Item No. 380. The text on the box said: "The pieced poppy is all straight sewing, the sort that may be run up on the sewing machine, while the bottom half of the block has two leaves and a stem that whips down by hand." The catalog said: "The original was gorgeous in two values of red, a flame and a scarlet, for the poppy. Then a flower center of black, boil proof of course, two values of the poppy color and green appliqué. For an entire quilt top, 5½ blocks long by 5 wide— or about 72 inches by 80 inches after all the seams are off— you will require nine and one-third yards. We select this for

you in beautiful 80 square cambric finish material with all the pieces ready cut as No. 380C." The kit came in a variety of color themes, although the scarlet/orange was the most popular.

McKim Studios and the publication of Ruby's book created a unique niche during the Depression. Women were looking for inexpensive projects they could make themselves to beautify their homes and give as presents. The success of their business allowed Arthur and Ruby, with daughters Betty and Marilyn, to travel to Europe in 1931. Before they left for the trip, they purchased a big stone house next door to McKim Studios.

The trip, however, was not just for fun. They attended expositions in Belgium and Paris. When they visited the French Colonial Exposition, they discovered exhibits of native handiwork from countries all around the world. Ten-year-old daughter Marilyn was enchanted by the dolls dressed in their native costumes, and several were purchased as souvenirs. These dolls proved to be the first seeds for a new direction for their business.

The world was changing. People were beginning to be more interested in buying ready-made quilts, rather than patterns and supplies. The McKims started to feature dolls occasionally in their catalogs.

The 1930s was the transition decade for the McKims, starting with the arrival of their son, Kim, in 1933. In addition to the changes in demand for quilt-related products, McKim Studios had grown so large that it was necessary to outsource jobs. Since they could not ensure quality control, McKim Studios began the metamorphosis into Kimport Dolls in 1935.

Kim and Barbara were married in 1953. Soon after, his parents began taking money out of his paycheck to purchase Kimport Dolls for him. They had been grooming him for this all his life, and he would run Kimport Dolls until its closing in 1985. He died three years later.

Arthur had died on Father's Day, June 18, 1967. Their stone house was sold when Ruby moved into a nursing home.

She died in 1976, having made a significant contribution to the world of quilts through her designs and illustrations. She was also an incredible businesswoman, well ahead of her time.

After working as an art director at a small advertising agency, Merrily McKim Tuohey did freelance work under the name McKim-Tuohey Studio, named in honor of the connection with her grandmother. Learning about her grandmother's past inspired Merrily to revive McKim Studios. She has created a website that offers a wide variety of Ruby's patterns. Eventually, there will be a photo gallery of quilts, as well as quilt kits and other McKim items. A section on the website for quilt historians and researchers will include documentation of patterns, articles written by and about Ruby, as well as the original McKim Studios catalogs and marketing materials. Another of Merrily's websites features all the patterns and text from the 1931 edition *One Hundred and One Patchwork Patterns,* which are available to download for free.

Merrily has also assembled a board of advisors for the Ruby Short McKim Collaborative—Janette Dwyer, Christina Fullerton Jones (Ruby's eldest grandchild), Carol Keller, Donna Kooistra, Barbara Wells, and Rose Marie Werner—to provide support. "Our passion for Ruby Short McKim has brought us together. Our mission is to champion her life's work and create an honorable tribute to her amazing life," says her granddaughter Merrily. 🖎

# A BLESSING
# AND AN AFFIRMATION

*Note: Some names have been omitted to respect the Amish need for privacy.*

As it is in many Amish families, quiltmaking was an important tradition for Carol Honderich's mother, aunts, and grandmothers, and they all enjoyed it. A quilt could often be found in a large frame set up in the house, and by the time she was ten years old, Carol already considered herself to be a quiltmaker.

Carol remembers the red, white, and blue Stars and Cubes quilt that was used occasionally on her parents' bed, but she does not remember ever being told the story behind the quilt. After her grandmother's death in 1985 at the age of eighty-eight, Carol began to research her grandmother's life. She created a timeline so she could better understand the important events

**Stars and Cubes**
Made by Susanna "Susie" Schrock (1896–1985)
1947
70 x 80 inches
Cotton; hand pieced and hand quilted
*Collection of Carol Honderich, photo by Carol Honderich*

her grandmother faced, her age at the time of each event, and the other conditions of her life. This helped Carol understand a great deal about her grandmother and also shed light on the circumstances of her father's upbringing. Her father, Joseph, had never shared much about his childhood with her.

In August 1896, Carol's grandmother, Susanna "Susie" Schrock, was born. She was the eighth of thirteen children born into an Amish family in Arthur, Illinois. In 1918, at the age of twenty-two, she married George Helmuth, who was two years older. World War I had postponed their marriage. During the war, George was stationed at a military base in Michigan where, as a young Amish man, he maintained a status of conscientious objector (CO). There were no provisions for conscientious objectors at this time, such as the Civilian Public Service (CPC) or 1-W status available to later generations of Amish men and other conscientious objectors.

George spoke the Pennsylvania Dutch dialect of German, which did not endear him to his military peers in a war with Germany. Like many other Amish men, his CO status caused him considerable physical and mental abuse at the hands of military personnel. The stories George shared about this time would be remembered by his oldest son, Joseph, long after George was gone and would greatly influence Joseph's decisions regarding his own military involvement in World War II.

After George and Susie married, they lived on a large farm owned by George's father. Susie enjoyed gardening, canning, and sewing for her family. She learned how to quilt and enjoyed quilting with the women in her community. Their family grew quickly. Their first child, a daughter, was born in December

1918, followed by another daughter in January 1920. Joseph, who was named after Susie's father, was born in April 1922. In August 1923, another son was born, and their last daughter was born in April 1926. During the Great Depression, even the frugal lifestyle of the Amish was severely tested. By 1932, though, the economy was beginning to stabilize, and life was improving for them. Later in her life, Susie would share that she felt her family was complete at this point.

In October 1932, George suffered a serious head injury in a farm accident. While he was able to make it home, he quickly fell into a coma. Later that night, with Susie and their children gathered around his bedside, he died.

Even with all the children participating, the work of the large farm was more than Susie could handle. She decided to sell the livestock and move to a smaller farm owned by her father. For two years, Susie struggled to provide for her children. Her biggest fear was that something would happen to her, and she would be unable to care for them. Even within the Amish community, she had few places to turn to for help.

Jacob Schlabach of LaGrange County, Indiana, had been married and widowed twice and was father of seven children. In addition, his second wife had been a widow with three children from her previous marriage, so Jacob had ten motherless children to care for, three of whom had lost both of their parents. Jacob's oldest stepdaughter, still a child herself, was now raising the younger children and caring for the home.

Jacob had fallen on hard times, losing not only his wife but also his farm. When Jacob heard about Susie, it did not take him long to decide to travel to Illinois to court her. No one knows how long the courtship lasted or when Susie finally agreed to marry Jacob, but in February 1935, at age thirty-nine, she did. In the Amish community, marriage provided a sense of security, and there was also status for being a wife and mother. Susie also brought much-needed cash into the relationship, which would help to buy a new farm. However, marrying Jacob meant leaving her home, her family, and the community that she had known her entire life and moving nearly 300 miles away. It also meant combining four sets of siblings—fifteen children—all still living at home. Susie knew from personal experience how much energy and resources such a large family required.

Of course, families of this size were not unusual in the Amish community, where children are viewed as an asset and gift from God, but for Susie's children, the move could not have been easy. Her son Joseph was a sensitive child and only twelve years old when the move happened. Susie did what she could to comfort him during this difficult transition. However, Jacob and Susie then started having children of their own. Their first son was born in January 1936, followed by another in February 1937. Their daughter (born in August 1938) was a very weak and fragile infant who also had Down syndrome. The family did all they could to care for her. Against all odds, she survived and lived to be seventy years old, dying in 2008. Tragedy struck again in January 1940 when a son was stillborn. Their last child, a daughter, was born in November 1941, when Susie was forty-five years old.

In addition to farming, Jacob ran a sawmill business from his home, which provided employment for his nine sons. At the age of sixteen, Joseph finished school and went to work for his stepfather. (Amish children only study until eighth grade.) When the Japanese bombed Pearl Harbor, twenty-year-old Joseph knew it was just a matter of time before he would be drafted if he did not enlist first.

Many of the Amish avoided military service by applying for farm deferments or hardship deferments. Some opted for civil service programs. Joseph's feelings toward the Amish church were ambiguous, so he did not wish to hide behind the church to avoid military service. Joseph also remembered his father's stories about serving in the military as a conscientious objector. He decided to take advantage of the privileges gained by being an enlisted man. During the next five years, he was stationed in Kansas, England, Germany, and Chicago, where he worked as a laboratory assistant and a medic. He found Army life afforded him more opportunities than his Amish life, so he re-enlisted. He did not return home until March 1947.

The Amish believe in shunning things of the world, including politics and military involvement, and yet the relief and joy that the war was over were also experienced by many of the Amish. Susie's own pride for her son and his contribution to the war effort was not easily expressed in words or demonstrations, so she did what she could: She made him a quilt.

Amish quilts of 1940 LaGrange County were frequently made with a light background, unlike the Pennsylvania Amish quilts, which were generally made with dark fabrics. In the 1930s and 1940s, some Amish communities did not approve of purchasing new fabric for quiltmaking, but this was not the case with the Amish quiltmakers in LaGrange County, who often purchased fabrics specifically for the making of a quilt. It was obvious that Susie's quilt was made from yardage purchased for a quilt. The white background was all cut from the same fabric. She used this white background to display the bright red and blue eight-pointed stars. The red and blue fabrics used show no variation in dye lot from piece to piece. The back of the quilt was also made from all the same fabric. The binding matches the blue in the stars.

Susie chose the pattern called Stars and Cubes to create the 70-inch by 80-inch quilt. It was a somewhat difficult pattern to piece, but she sewed it skillfully on her treadle sewing machine. She used cotton batting and a feather and crosshatch quilting design. The quilting was done by hand using ten stitches to the inch.

In August 1947, the quilt became a wedding gift for Joseph and his bride, Mary. Joseph's love for Mary kept him in the Amish faith, but five years into their marriage, they became Mennonites. The Amish and Mennonite churches still share the same beliefs concerning baptism, nonresistance, and basic Bible doctrines. They differ in matters of dress, technology, language, form of worship, and interpretation of the Bible. The Mennonites tend to be less conservative. Most Mennonites have relaxed dress codes and have gotten away from farm-related occupations. While Old Order Mennonites still drive their all-black carriages, most Mennonite groups do permit the use of cars and electricity. The five years that Joseph had spent in the world had, indeed, changed him.

Mary and Joseph would have four daughters: Dolores, Carol, Anita, and Elaine. The sisters see their father's traits of self-sufficiency, creativity, stubbornness, and risk taking in themselves. Dolores became a registered nurse and practiced for a number of years before returning to school to earn a degree in graphic design. She now owns a design business. Carol is a quiltmaker, quilt designer, and teacher and works as an event facilitator for Mennonite Church USA. Anita is a doctor in obstetrics and gynecology. Elaine is a teacher primarily providing services for severely disabled preschool kids.

In his lifetime, Joseph rarely worked for anyone else but owned his own businesses, selling cars and recreational vehicle parts and manufacturing recreational vehicles. He designed and built a beautiful large home, but lost it to the bank when the recreational vehicles market plummeted in the 1970s.

Joseph's wife, Mary, initially thought the quilt was nice special because of the circumstances, but basically just a bed cover. A quiltmaker herself, she made quilts for all of her children to use. Over the years, the quilt became a treasured possession, especially after the death of her mother-in-law, and even more so after Joseph died. In spring 2010, when Mary moved from her home to a small retirement apartment, her daughter Carol asked for the quilt, with the promise to love and care for it. It was given to her. Of all Mary's children, Carol was the only quiltmaker and the person who took an interest in the quilt.

"My grandmother wanted to do something special for my dad. I believe not only to honor his service in the military, but to let him know that she was proud of him and recognized what his life had been like in those fifteen years between the death of his father and his marriage to my mother." And while there are many quilts in the family, for Carol this one will always be special. ᴎ

# A GIFT FOR ELEANOR

ale Rosengarten remembers the incredible family
jewelry Judith Shanks was wearing the first time
the two women met at the Jewish Historical Society
in Columbia, South Carolina, in 1999. Judith remembers
feeling an instant connection with Dale. Dale was curating
the exhibition *A Portion of the People: Three Hundred Years
of Southern Jewish Life.* She had been working on it for four
years. The show's title and focus came from a letter sent to
then-U.S. Secretary of State James Monroe in 1816 by Isaac
Harby, protesting the removal of Mordecai Manuel Noah as
consul to Tunis. "[Jews] are by no means to be considered as
a religious sect, tolerated by the government," Harby wrote.
"They constitute a portion of the People. They are, in every
respect, woven in and compacted with the citizens of the

---

**Album quilt**
Made for Eleanor Israel Solomons (née Joseph, 1794–1856) by various contributors,
    South Carolina
Blocks fabricated 1851–1854
102 x 113 inches
Chintz and calico on muslin; pieced and appliquéd
Displayed in the exhibition *A Portion of the People: Three Hundred Years of Southern Jewish
    Life* and included in the exhibition's catalog published by University of South Carolina
    Press, 2002
*Collection of Judith W. Shanks, photo by Stephen Halperson, Tisara Photography*

Republic." The exhibition would include a significant group of objects and documentation of the people and circumstances that produced them. After receiving her Ph.D. from Harvard University, Dale was hired by the College of Charleston in 1995 as curator of the Jewish Heritage Collection, which eventually led to the exhibition.

Shortly after the meeting, Judith became one of Dale's research associates. In addition to helping find objects for the exhibition, Judith also provided a Southern point of view (she grew up in Alabama) to balance Dale's natural tendencies as a "come-here" from the North (she was originally from New York City).

Judith shared with Dale that she had a great uncle, Henry A. Alexander Sr., who had spent his life chronicling the family history. Henry A. Alexander Jr., of Eugene, Oregon, now deceased, made available his father's collection for research and subsequently gave the collection to Judith. His research would prove invaluable. Judith and Dale also visited Judith's uncle Cecil Alexander to collect information for their upcoming exhibit.

It was during their visit to Cecil Alexander's home in Atlanta, Georgia, that Dale saw a quilt made for Eleanor Solomons in the early 1850s. The pieced and appliquéd chintz and calico quilt was in bad shape, and sometime in its past, a pink ruffle had been added to make it fit a bed. Cecil agreed to loan the quilt for the exhibition, and a grant provided by the Jewish Heritage Collection would allow Elizabeth Ingber of Bayside, New York, to conserve the quilt. Cecil would eventually give the quilt to Judith.

Eleanor Joseph, one of Sarah Judith Jaduh and Lizar Joseph's eight children, was born in 1794 in the hamlet of Black Mingo, South Carolina, and grew up in Georgetown. Eleanor's mother was originally from Philadelphia, and her father was born in Mannheim, Germany. Lizar became a salt merchant and wharf owner in the port of Georgetown.

South Carolina was the first state to grant Jews the right to vote. In 1800, approximately two thousand Jews lived in South Carolina, more than in any other state, and the Jewish business class dominated civic and cultural life in Georgetown particularly. In 1814, at the age of nineteen, Eleanor married Israel Solomons. He was forty-four. Born in Amsterdam, Israel had tried to make a living in South America and the West Indies before immigrating to South Carolina. Throughout his life, he was plagued by financial difficulties. When he died in 1830, he left Eleanor and their eight surviving children destitute.

In the early 1850s, Eleanor moved from Georgetown to Savannah to live with her son Lizar and his wife, Perla. Charlotte Joseph, Eleanor's younger sister, organized the making of an album quilt as a gift and remembrance of family and friends for Eleanor. Family and friends, women and girls, Jews and gentiles, sewed sixty-three blocks that were then pieced together. The blocks were appliquéd or pieced onto muslin. Some of the designs in the individual blocks were trimmed with crocheted braid, some with embroidery. The motif of repeating hexagons used in the quilt was popularized by *Godey's Lady's Book*, which promoted the technique of cutting out paper templates, basting fabric onto the paper, then sewing the pieces together.

Among Henry Alexander Sr.'s papers was a letter that identified the creators of each block. Most of the makers were identified by inscriptions, inked in black by Eleanor. Many are too faded to read now, but were legible nearly sixty years ago when they were transcribed and recorded by Henry. Henry was the author of *Notes on the Alexander Family of South Carolina and Georgia and connections, 1651–1954*, self published in 1954 in Georgia.

The contributors to the quilt lived mainly in South Carolina and Georgia, but cousins living as far away as New York also made blocks. The center block with a peacock and eagles is signed by "C," who might be Eleanor's sister, Charlotte Joseph. One block was made by six-year-old Cecilia Solomons, Eleanor's granddaughter and adopted daughter of Lizar and Perla Solomons. She wrote on her block, "To 'Grandma' from Cecilia 6 years old." Young Cecilia's aunt, also named Cecilia Solomons, who lived near Lizar and Perla in Savannah, was an accomplished needleworker from the time she was fourteen (last row, center block). Cecilia's mother, Rebecca Mose, also contributed a block, a seven-point star (second row, four from the left).

The quilt also includes a block sewn by one of Eleanor's slaves, named Rinah (third row, three from the right). The inscription on the block reads "My servant Rinah." As valuable property, Rinah and her children were mortgaged more than once by Eleanor's husband, Israel Solomons. Whether to protect their investment, or from motives of the heart, the Solomons saw to it that Rinah's children received medical attention. In 1830, the year Israel died, one of Rinah's daughters was under a doctor's care for almost three weeks. The bill was sixty dollars, or about a year's gross income for a typical slave. Despite being destitute herself, Eleanor, as "Administrix" of her husband's estate, paid the bill. After the Civil War, Rinah remained a servant in the household of Eleanor's daughter, Sarah. The surname(s) taken by Rinah and her children upon emancipation are unknown.

Eleanor Solomons died in 1856. The quilt stayed in the family until it was given to Eleanor's great-great-great-granddaughter, Judith Shanks. The quilt was first displayed as part of *A Portion of the People: Three Hundred Years of Southern Jewish Life* when the exhibit opened at the McKissick Museum in Columbia, South Carolina, in January 2002. The exhibition with its catalog, a collaboration between Dale Rosengarten and her husband, Theodore (a teacher, writer, and community activist), had ultimately taken seven years of work to come to fruition.

The exhibition traveled to the Gibbes Museum of Art in Charleston, South Carolina, and the Yeshiva University Museum, Center for Jewish History in New York City. The tour ended in November 2003 at the Levine Museum of the New South in Charlotte, North Carolina. In the process of identifying material for the exhibit, Dale and her colleagues in College of Charleston's Special Collections Department developed a major Jewish archives, for which she was awarded the first Governor's Archives Award in 2003.

Eleanor's quilt is now with Judith, who hopes to donate it one day to a South Carolina institution so that it can be preserved and shared with future generations. ✍

# THE WESTWARD TRAIL OF SARAH SNOUFFER'S QUILT

I t had been a long day at the Woodin Wheel Antiques Shop in Kalona, Iowa, with all the preparations for the annual Kalona Quilt Show and Sale. Marilyn Woodin, the shop's owner and founder of the sale, was thoroughly tired by the time a middle-aged woman walked in carrying a quilt. Registration for the sale was closed, but the woman, who introduced herself as Donna Shadden, pleaded for her quilt to be included. Donna explained that the quilt had been discovered in a storage shed behind a house in Iowa, where it had been for years and perhaps decades. She also shared names of some of the people who had possession of the quilt, including a Sarah Baer.

When Marilyn asked the price, she was shocked by the amount. "I don't think it will sell," she said, but she agreed to

---

*Baby*
Feathered Star
Maker unknown, Maryland
Circa 1825–1840
Cotton; hand pieced and hand quilted
*Collection of Marilyn Woodin, photo by Mary V. Zielinski*

try. Without really looking at the entire quilt, she carried it to the back of the store for safekeeping. A little later, it occurred to her that she really should take a look at it. When she opened it, her heart stopped. Before her was a red and green pieced Feather Star on a white background with a beautiful red and green chintz border. The hand quilting was ten to twelve stitches per inch. Not only was it beautiful, but it was in pristine condition. It seemed it had never been used or laundered. Marilyn quickly dropped everything that she was doing and ran to the bank to get a loan to purchase the quilt.

After Marilyn bought the quilt, Donna sent her a letter.

January 25, 1988

Dear Marilyn:

I was way off base with the name Baer. Although the name is in our lineage, it is not one connected to the quilt as the enclosed note states.

Lucy Snouffer was my grandmother's unmarried sister. She came to live with my Grandmother Laub in Denison, Iowa in 1911. Laub is a very prominent name in Denison's history.

When my parents, Mr. and Mrs. Henry Clay Laub, had to break up my grandmother's home, we received the quilt with many other beautiful antiques. My mother found this quilt and another in a trunk in a storage shed in the backyard.

When my mother saw it she knew it had to be old and perhaps had some value. She rescued it and, when I had to dispose of my mother's things, the quilt came to me. I had no space to keep the quilt and thought it should be somewhere it would be cared for properly and possibly enjoyed by others.

Hopefully it has found its home with you.

Your friend,

Donna Shadden

Nodaway, Iowa

A note attached to the quilt had multiple contributions. First, "This quilt is 164 165 yrs old" was written in ink, and someone had typed, "This quilt was made in Frederick County, Maryland, in 1820, by Sarah Rannabargar Snouffer. The quilt was brought to Missouri in 1850 by W. H. Snouffer. In 1911 it was brought to Iowa by Miss Lucy Snouffer." At the top of the note, written in ballpoint pen: "I believe Frederick County, Maryland is no [sic] what is Washington D. C." Marilyn believes Donna may have written it. The number of years indicated seems to imply that the first two parts of the note were written in 1985.

The family believes the quilt was made by Sarah Elizabeth Snouffer Belt. Sarah was born on December 10, 1829, in Frederick County, Maryland. (Ranneberger was Sarah's mother's maiden name.) She married Dr. James Belt in 1854 at the residence of Henry Snouffer near Licksville, Maryland. Following their marriage, they moved to Napoleon, Missouri. An 1881 book on Lafayette County, Missouri, however, lists 1851 as the year James initially arrived in Missouri. It is possible that he came to Missouri as a bachelor to establish his medical and drugstore business, then went back to Maryland to marry Sarah.

We do know a few details about their life together. James opened the first drugstore in Napoleon, which was operated in connection with his medical practice. Together, James and Sarah had eight children, born between 1855 and 1872. In the 1910 census, we find them living with two of their children, James Alfred and Florence (forty-five and forty-nine years old), in Oklahoma City, Oklahoma. James died in 1916 at the age of ninety-five, and Sarah followed him in 1917 at the age of eighty-eight.

William Henry Snouffer was Sarah's younger brother. William married another Sarah (Bear/Baer) in 1851 in Carrollton Manor, Maryland. Their first three children were born in Maryland, but died in infancy. Two of their children, daughters, were buried in 1854 at the Olde Thomas Family Burial Grounds in Point of Rock, Maryland. Their fourth child, William Henry Snouffer Jr., was born in Napoleon, Missouri, in 1856, so sometime between 1854 and 1856 the family moved to Missouri.

According to the note, the quilt was passed from Sarah to her brother William and then to William's daughter Lucy Snouffer. Lucy was born in Napoleon in 1864 and was William and Sarah's seventh child. Lucy never married. Her obituary in the *Denison Bulletin*, February 29, 1940, states that she moved permanently to Iowa in 1901. She lived in her sister Mary's home along with her unmarried brother James until her death on February 25, 1940, after which time, the quilt passed to Mary.

Mary was two years younger than Lucy, and, according to Mary's obituary in the *Denison Bulletin*, she came to Denison,

Iowa, when she was "about twenty" in 1886. She married Henry Laub in 1898, which caused quite a scandal. She was Henry's second wife. His first wife, Lydia Baer Laub, died in 1886, and Lydia was Sarah Baer Snouffer's sister, so Mary had married her uncle! Henry was also forty-two years older than Mary.

The town was once again up in arms when their child, Henry Clay Laub Jr., was born in 1899. Henry Sr. died in 1910 following a long illness. The writer of Henry's obituary in the *Denison Review* not so subtly chastised the Denison community for their opinions of Henry's marriage to Mary when he wrote,

We recognize the custom, which apparently is inexorable, that these things shall come after death and not before, but we are inclined to believe that it would be better if the custom should be relaxed enough to recognize sacrifices made and devotion to duty exhibited while one is still among the living. A splendid illustration is furnished in this case in the complete concentration and devotion of the wife during the long and serious illness of her husband and while his condition was such that he was practically unable to help himself. For many long months, and even years, this wife, prompted by the love which she bore her husband, with cheerfulness, devoted her life to making him comfortable and happy. It may be said that it was her duty to do all that she did, and this may be conceded, and yet it is not always the case that duty is discharged as it was in this instance. Mrs. Laub, in her complete devotion to duty, is entitled to and should receive the esteem and affection in this community.

Mary lived in her home in Denison until September 1944, when she moved in with her son in Council Bluffs, Iowa. She died in 1949. When her daughter-in-law, Alice, was going through her possessions after her death, she found two quilts in a trunk in a storage shed and rescued them.

Mary's son, Henry, married Alice Hawe in 1926. They lived in Denison before moving to Council Bluffs in 1943.

They had two children, Henry Clay Laub III and Donna Rae. Since the note was probably written in 1985 while Alice owned the quilt, we can speculate that she wrote the two original entries on the note. She would have been eighty-seven years old at that time. Henry Jr. died in 1971, and when Alice died in 1987, Donna inherited the quilt. Donna is the one who sold the quilt to Marilyn.

The quilt became one of Marilyn's favorites in her collection and a prized possession, so much so that she named the quilt *Baby* because she has always treated the quilt just like a baby. It is carefully wrapped in a sheet whenever Marilyn takes it places, and it has its own special drawer for storage. It is cared for, loved, and pampered.

In 1988, Marilyn hosted a quilt seminar and invited Barbara Brackman to give a lecture. Marilyn could not resist showing the quilt to Barbara. At the time, Barbara was writing her book *Clues in the Calico: A Guide to Identifying and Dating Antique Quilts* (EPM Publications, Inc., 1989), and she asked if she could include Marilyn's quilt in her book. Of course, Marilyn agreed, and the quilt was featured in full color on page 8.

> *Marilyn named the quilt* Baby *because she has always treated the quilt just like a baby.*

Being a quilt historian, Marilyn knew the importance of having her quilts appraised. In the early 1990s, a professional appraiser dated the making of the quilt to 1825–1840 and confirmed that acquiring a loan for the quilt was worth it.

When Marilyn's husband became ill, she sold her store. Before she "retired," she donated thirty-two quilts from her private collection to the Kalona Historical Society in exchange for a light- and humidity-controlled building for a textile museum. In addition, she would curate the museum in a volunteer capacity as long as she was able. This is how the Kalona Quilt and Textile Museum was created in 2000. The museum has nearly four hundred quilts in its collection now. *Baby* is not one of them yet.

The connections to the Snouffer clan would continue. A woman named Karen Knecht had caught the genealogy bug. It was a good diversion for her since she had quit her job in order to care for her mother, who had Alzheimer's. It also provided opportunities to connect with her mother because her mother loved looking at all the photographs Karen was collecting for her family notebook.

One day in 2004, while Karen was poking around the Internet searching for anything related to "Snouffer," she was led to Barbara Brackman's book, *Clues in the Calico*, on Amazon. The "Look Inside" feature allowed her to see the page with the quilt and the notation under the quilt, which gave information on who owned it—Woodin Wheel Antiques. Another quick search gave Karen a name and address. She wrote a letter to Marilyn saying, "I think you have a quilt that is part of my family's history. Would you be willing to correspond with me?" It turned out that Donna was Karen's cousin.

Marilyn did correspond with Karen and eventually gave her the original note that was attached to the quilt and letter from Donna for her family notebook. Karen, with the help of her cousin, Bill Snouffer of Portland, Oregon, would gather genealogy information on the people mentioned in the note and share this information with Marilyn. They titled it *The Westward Trail of Sarah Snouffer's Quilt*. Bill and two other family members also made arrangements to visit and photograph the quilt. Because of the love and care that Marilyn had provided for their family's quilt, she was invited to the Snouffer family reunion in 2010 and made an honorary Snouffer.

We will probably never know for sure who made the quilt, or whether it was made as a wedding or a parting gift by Sarah Snouffer Belt for her brother William, as the family now believes, or by someone else. We do know that it must have been considered special since it was neither used nor laundered, and we also know that it will always be Marilyn's *Baby*. ❧

# I WILL

One hot August day in 1995, Janette Dwyer and her sister, Jeanne Mirocha, were looking for something to do together. While perusing the *Henry County Advertizer*, a local circular, they came across an auction that was being held about twenty miles away in Cambridge, Illinois, and decided it might be fun. They arrived at the sale early to get a sense of what was there, and a very dirty, scrappy quilt that was rolled up, stuck in a box, and placed under a table caught Janette's eye. When she unrolled the quilt to get a better look, she discovered it was a Postage Stamp style quilt with squares of fabrics from 1870 to 1930. She was "pretty sure" she wanted the quilt.

Janette had started making quilts in 1983 while she was a senior in high school. Her neighbor, Dorothy Jodts, taught her, and she was instantly hooked. The quilt she found at the

---

**Postage Stamp**
Maker unknown, Illinois
Circa 1932
76 x 78 inches
Cotton fabrics from 1890–1930; hand pieced and hand quilted
An entry in the 1933 World's Fair Century of Progress International Exposition,
    Sears Quilt Contest in Chicago, Illinois
*Collection of Janette Dywer, photo by Tracy Diehl*

auction was part of the estate of Harry Ortt, who had been born in Guthrie, Iowa, in 1907. He had moved to East Moline, Illinois, sometime in the 1930s. He had been married twice but had no children. The estate sale was court appointed since he did not have any heirs, so there was no one to answer questions about the quilt—who had made it, when, or where.

There were about a dozen quilts and quilt tops for sale. When "the" quilt came up for sale, Janette quickly won with a bid of $24. The auctioneer then announced, "Since you're the top bidder, you get to choose as many quilts and tops as you want to purchase at your bid price." In addition to the Postage Stamp style quilt, Janette decided to buy a quilt top that had alternating rows of five-inch squares of 1940s fabric and rows of chevrons in 1880s fabric as well as a primitive appliqué Nine Patch quilt, circa 1880. Some of the fabric in the Nine Patch had tiny jockey caps and riding crops, and some of the appliqué pieces were the outline of a child's hand, with one hand bearing initials and another (on the opposite side of the quilt) holding the words *Zeb's Hand* sewn in red embroidery floss. "I love looking at this quilt and just wishing that it could tell me of the journey of its quilt life before it got into my hands," says Janette.

When Janette got back to her seat, she opened the quilt that had first caught her eye. Once she got beyond how dirty the quilt was (it would take eight cleanings to restore it), she was amazed by her newfound treasure. The 76-inch by 78-inch scrap quilt comprised 1½-inch squares of a variety of fabrics from approximately 1890 to 1930. Looking closer, she saw, spelled out in block letters down the right side, the word *visitor*, and down the left side was the word *welcome.* In the center of the quilt, outlined in blue, was a dove or an eagle, and inside it were the words *I will*. Looking even closer, she discovered the words *Century of Progress Exhibition, 1933, Chicago* and *Illinois*. There were also two red stars. It was minimally quilted and the batting was flannel. She knew she had to find out more.

Two weeks later, Janette took the quilt to a nearby quilt shop. She was directed to the book *Patchwork Souvenirs of the 1933 World's Fair* by Merikay Waldvogel and Barbara Brackman (Rutledge Hill Press, 1993), which she purchased and read cover to cover. She also learned that an exhibition of thirty of the top prize winning quilts, curated by Merikay and Barbara, would be on display in Janesville, Wisconsin, in

> *"I love looking at this quilt and just wishing that it could tell me its journey."*

just three weeks. Merikay and Barbara would also be giving a lecture.

The 1933 World's Fair Century of Progress International Exposition, with the Sears National Quilt Contest, was held in Chicago, Illinois. Chicago was celebrating its one hundredth birthday, and one of the fair's themes was "From Wagon Wheels to Wings," meant to express the progress of the last one hundred years. The quilt contest was announced January 15, 1933 with the emphasis on submitting quilts that were original in design. The deadline was May 15, 1933. The contest's top prize was $1,000 (nearly $16,000 today). If a quilt was chosen as the winner and it had the words *Century of Progress* somewhere on it, Sears would give the winner an additional $200 in prize money.

Quilts were first judged at local Sears stores, then at the regional level, and finally in the competition at the fair. Local winners were awarded $5 to $10, and regional winners received as much as $200. A total of 24,878 entries were submitted. Sears estimated that the quiltmakers had spent 5,000,625 total hours in making their quilts for the contest. (It was figured that a quilt took an estimated 225 hours to construct, or about twenty-eight eight-hour days.) It was then calculated that the time was equal to 642 years or 234,875 days.

Janette decided to contact Merikay about her quilt, and Merikay asked her to bring the quilt to Janesville. The quilt was displayed and discussed during the lecture, and Merikay was able to explain some of the symbolism in the quilt. The two red stars represented the stars on the Chicago flag. The words *I will* in the center of the yellow background of the bird came from the official motto of the fair, "I will overcome all obstacles," eventually shortened to "I will." The two lines that come down diagonally and then in a straight line into a "Y" suggest the spot where the two rivers come together in Chicago.

At this time, Merikay and Barbara were also on a mission to document as many Century of Progress quilts as they could find. Janette's quilt was documented as number 160 of the quilts they had located. They are still documenting Century of Progress quilts as they come their way.

In September 2003, a man left a message on Janette's answering machine, saying, "I have a client who has a quilt that I think might be of interest to you. If you would come down to the auction tomorrow, I'll personally show it to you." Janette and her husband, Mike, have a farm, and the corn was not dry enough to harvest yet, so Janette had an unexpected day off. She decided to check out the estate sale in Gridley, Illinois.

When the man showed her the quilt, she could not pass up buying it. This time, the bidding went on for a while until it reached $275, and once again Janette was the top bidder. When Janette asked the man how he had found her, he said that he had kept a newspaper article written about the Century of Progress quilt she owned.

Janette contacted the family that had owned her latest quilt to learn more about the quilt and its maker. The maker's daughter shared that the quilt had been created by Irene Schramm, who had been born and lived her entire life in Gridley. She died in 1974 at the age of eighty-one. In addition to making quilts, Irene loved to write letters. She was known as "Grandma Schramm" to the hundreds of servicemen with whom she corresponded. Her quilt was from a Ruby Short McKim series design called *State Flowers*. Irene had clipped the patterns out of the *Pantagraph*, a Bloomington, Illinois, newspaper. (She had also been a Gridley reporter for the *Pantagraph*.)

*Irene must have loved competitions*, thought Janette. The quilt Janette bought had been entered in the State Flower Quilt Contest. The top prize was $500, and all the quilts had to use Ruby Short McKim's state flower quilt patterns. (Newspapers began printing the patterns in 1931.) Quilts were judged first in cities, then nationally in Washington, D.C., in 1932. Then Irene was clever enough to turn around five months later, add a top section to the quilt with the words

*Century of Progress 1933*, and enter it in the World's Fair quilt contest. Affixed to the quilt was also a blue ribbon that read "Fall Festival and Colt Show, Gridley, Illinois, August 29–31, 1940," a third contest.

"So I am the proud owner of two Century of Progress quilts. I could have died happy if I had owned just one!" says Janette.

Janette still kicks herself for not buying what would have been her first Century of Progress quilt, though she knew nothing about the Century of Progress contest at the time. Early in 1995, when she was working at the Quilt Quarters, a woman brought in a quilt. She wanted to sell it for $300 and wondered if Janette would be interested in purchasing it. It had a little gold ribbon with the words *Emma and Lena Neumann* on it. It had been a third place regional winner in the contest.

Emma and Lena Neumann are third cousins of Janette's mom. Both ladies had never married, so when they passed away, the quilt was given to their sister. When she died, the quilt was passed to her daughter, and the daughter was the one who brought the quilt into the shop. Janette didn't purchase it, so the woman ended up taking the quilt to a local antique shop in town. The quilt was purchased by the seller's first cousin. "I could have owned three, three Century of Progress quilts! I guess I just have to let that one go," says Janette with a sigh.

While Janette was visiting her friend Angie Marshall in 2008, Angie suggested that there might be some quilts Janette would like on eBay. Since Angie was a seasoned eBay buyer, Janette thought, *Why not give it a try?* They decided to see if they could find anything by searching for "Century of Progress." Jackpot! The search produced a 1933 Chicago World's Fair coverlet woven in beige and rust with symbols of the fair. With Angie doing the bidding, Janette was now the proud owner of the coverlet and had made her first purchase on eBay.

She contacted the owner of the coverlet, who kindly provided her with this information:

> We come from Michigan, a small farming town. My aunt and uncle were married in 1933. Fixed marriage between two families, imagine that! Anyway, being very young and not really knowing each other, they were scared like heck to go off on a honeymoon together. They decided on Chicago, the World's Fair. There they got to know each other and they bought this coverlet as a reminder of the wonderful time they had had. They were married 62 years. After their passing, sad as could be, we had an estate sale. This blanket was part of it, but no one bought it. Imagine that, again, so I took it home. Now in my later years also, I wonder, why should I keep such a treasure put away in the cedar closet? I am so very happy it found a good home. Thanks so much for treasuring it.

The year 2005 was a turning point for Janette. She and Mike were farmers first, but there had been a drought that year, and they only harvested half a corn crop. Her quilt shop, Quilt Quarters, which she had purchased in 1999, was fun but a lot of work. It also did not provide enough income. When no one accepted the offer to purchase it, Janette closed the doors. Becoming an appraiser had always been a dream, so Janette decided it was time. In 2008, the dream became a reality. She also gives lectures centered on the more than 200 antique quilts in her collection, including her prized Century of Progress quilts. "That chance meeting with that wonderful quilt on that Sunday afternoon in 1995 was a life-changing experience for me. And it all began with one word—SOLD!" ❧

# ACKNOWLEDGMENTS

First, I need to thank Spike Gillespie, who set me on this path. I hope one day to repay her. I've discovered that writing a book is a true labor of love. I hope that as you read, you will feel as if you know the people in these stories because if you do, I know I've done my job. Of course, this would not have been possible without the sharing and open hearts of the people who made the discoveries: Karen Alexander, Delores Hamilton, Bill Volckening, Heather Lair, Sandy Bartelsmeyer, John Tracy, Leba Wine, Janine Jannière, Dee Adams, Matt Arnett, Dawn Goldsmith, Sarah Mantegna, Shelly Zegart, Linda Laird, Julie Silber, Rosalind Webster Perry, Janice Paine-Dawes, Barbara Burnham, Joe Cunningham, Lynne Perrella, Joan Laughlin, Linda Edkins Wyatt, Merrily Tuohey, Carol Honderich, Judith Shanks, Marilyn Woodin, and Janette Dwyer.

Then there are the people who helped me in my quest for information and stories. Amy Calder, reporter/columnist, *Morning Sentinel*, Waterville, Maine; Sunny Irvine Taylor; Linda Hein, reference assistant, Nebraska State Historical Society; Arline Crowley; LaVeda Cross; Don Reiter, principal, Waterville High School; Carolyn Ducey, International Quilt Center and Museum, University of Nebraska–Lincoln; Donna L. Kooistra; Wendell Zercher, Heritage Center of Lancaster County, Inc.; Stacy Hollander, American Folk Art Museum; Mary Klein, archivist, Diocese of Maryland; Connie Myers; Jennifer Utley; Barbara Brackman; Merikay Waldvogel; Clara Van Tassel; Jack Lindsey; Dale Rosengarten; Sharon Pinka; Elizabeth Cherry Owen; Alan Tremain; and Odille Joassin, Art Institute of Chicago, Textile Department.

Thanks to Dennis Griggs, who went above and beyond his responsibilities to get the photographs of the crazy quilt in Waterville, Maine.

A special thank-you goes to Carolyn Kolzow: One could not ask for a better cheerleader and someone who loves genealogy more. Thanks to my sons, Jeremiah and Nathaniel Stephan, and my daughter-in-law, Sang Meong Lee, for loving quilts and me. This book would not have been possible were it not for the support of my husband, Tom Stephan.

Last, but certainly not least, a huge thank-you to Voyageur Press for trusting me with this book and my editor, Melinda Keefe, for all her help.